# CHIPS from THE PONTIL

*By*
JOHN C. TIBBITTS

*Charter Member and First President
of The Antique Bottle Collectors Ass'n.*

*Editor of "The Pontil"*

*Published By*
John C. Tibbitts
Sacramento, California

*Printed By*
The Heirloom Press

Copyright, John C. Tibbitts 1963

All rights reserved. This book or any part thereof may not be reproduced without the permission of the publisher.

First Printing May, 1963
Second Printing June, 1966
Third Printing November, 1967
Fourth Printing January 1969
Fifth Printing December 1970

Cover Color Photo by Jim Palik

Standard Book Number 911508-01-5
Library of Congress Catalog Card Number 63-15946
Printed in the United States of America

## Bottle Collector's Lament

*When we spy a real old bottle just a hidin' neath the brush*
*And we run up all excited, gosh you ought to see us rush*
*Can you blame us for our cussin', as with care we pull it out*
*On the ground is yet the bottle, in our hand is just the spout;*

*Then when in a dump we're diggin', and a real old flask shows up*
*And we find our new found treasure tightly wedged beneath a cup*
*Can you blame us for our cussin', as we gently do our task*
*And find that cup is good as new, but had crushed our little flask;*

*Or roamin' 'round an old ghost town, and being 'neath its spell*
*You always run into one thing, that makes you want to yell*
*Can you blame us for this cussin', as we search the broken bits*
*And find those target shootin' fools were good and made all hits;*

*Well this could go on forever, but the woes are much the same*
*We bottlers keep on lookin' for those bottles full of fame*
*And maybe we are better off to find them fairly rare,*
*'Cause who would want old bottles if you found them everywhere?*

J C T

## Terminology

In order to standardize the terminology used in describing bottles, I suggest the following abbreviations (except for flasks). This, I feel, will be a big help in correspondence between collectors, between dealers and collectors, and between "horse-traders."

| ABBREVIATION | MEANING |
|---|---|
| ABM | Automatic Bottle Machine |
| BIMAL | Blown in mold, applied lip |
| BIMALOP | Blown in mold, applied lip, open pontil |
| BIMALGP | Blown in mold, applied lip, graphite pontil |
| FB | Freeblown |
| BIMALIS | Blown in mold, applied lip, inside screw lip |
| BIMALRB | Blown in mold, applied lip, round bottom |

Let's also underline (_____) any lettering embossed in the glass when describing a bottle; also use F = Front, L = Left Side, R = Right Side, and Bm = Bottom.

Can you picture this one?
BIMALOP 3¼" tall, rect., L — Doc't Marshall's, R — Snuff, aqua.

# FOREWORD

For those of you that have heard, I am writing a book on bottles — let's set the record straight. This is NOT it.

Everything in "Chips from the Pontil" is lifted directly from the notes I have been responsible for publishing and distributing since the start of the Antique Bottle Collector's Association.

The fact that some of it was written by the club secretary and the rest of it by myself, may be a little confusing. With this knowledge you should be able to understand the shifting from 1st to 3rd person. Frances Gwynne deserves the credit for most of the club notes portion.

Mrs. T. and I have had many requests for back issues of the Pontil and have mailed them out as long as they lasted. This has led us to believe "Chips" would be appreciated.

The material presented is necessarily not very orderly, but just the way it was written up month to month. There is a lot of information in it, but it does take a little reading.

The bottles pictured are all from our own collection and only part of them relate to the text.

## Birth of a Bottle Club
## or
## Is Ignorance Bliss?

On Thursday, October 15, 1959, Mr. J. C. Tibbitts, Acting Chairman, called the first meeting of a bottle collector's club to order with a welcome to his home, and an expression of pleasure that an idea long cherished by himself and his wife, as well as others present, had culminated in a get-together of this group of people with a common interest — old bottles.

Everyone present had already enjoyed browsing around four rooms of the house and the patio admiring the very interesting groups and rows of old and colorful bottles.

Mr. Tibbitts suggested each person express his ideas on what he hopes to get from the club, where and how often we should meet, officers, etc.

Mr. Tibbitts said one objective would be to try to work up a bibliography of informative literature. Everyone could bring the names of any books they know of that are available on the subject. He said he has found some information in copies of old magazines.

Mr. Larry Cope said if you have bottles with the name of a Glass Works on them you can find out in books how old they are. For instance, Libbey Owens started about 1800; before that it was just Libbey, so anything with just the name Libbey means it was made before 1800. McKesson's puts out a big book which is supposed to be available in libraries. It also shows the history of glass making from the time when bottles were hand blown and snapped off, to the modern machines. In the State Library you can look at old copies of Harper's and get some information. Mr. Tibbitts has indexed what he has been able to find in old editions.

Jackie and Lee Scroggin asked about the best method of cleaning old bottles. Some suggestions: sand and water; very strong acid; very fine steel wool, with tooth brush and piece of wire bent to get in corners; trisodium sulfate, bleach, detergent; shot and sharp gravel (gravel will not scratch glass). Someone suggested a machine for shaking the gravel. Mr. Tibbitts has started building one, but it runs too fast.

There was general discussion of places to hunt for old bottles; Placerville, Auburn, Rocklin, Loomis, Jackson, all are nearby towns that have old dumps. Carson City and Virginia City have larger areas for digging. In Sacramento, quite a few bottles are being found in the Redevelopment areas in the West End. It is interesting to note that the entire Solon Baseball field is built over an old city dump. Larry Cope said a couple of fellows who are making some good finds in the west end will open a bottle shop here soon.

Carl Cope brought a *Warner's Safe* (Plate # 8) bottle in from his car and passed it around for everyone to look at.

What about a name? Perhaps we can decide at the next meeting. ABC — Antique Bottle Collectors, was suggested by Carl Cope. Bring your ideas — Maybe we could give a bottle as a prize for the best suggestion.
*Frances Gwynne, Secretary*

Notes from your temporary chairman:
Objectives Decided On:
1. Exchange of information;
2. See other collections;
3. Trade duplicates;
4. Group trips;
5. Bring bottles to meetings and see if others can answer your questions;
6. Work up bibliography on Glass and Bottles;
7. Develop better cleaning methods;
8. Invite all bottle collectors to join club;
9. Research — find out the "Who, What, Why, When and Where" of glass factories, breweries, distilleries, bottling plants, etc.

Club Slogan (???):
Bigger better brown bitters bottles, beer bottles, blue bottles, and other beverage bottles or bust! *J. C. T.*

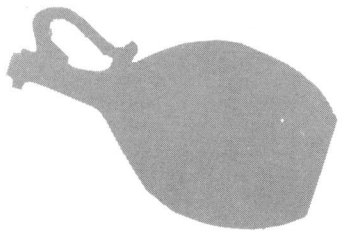

## II
## The "Christening"
## or We Become
## The Antique Bottle Collectors Association of California
## or
## ABCAC

A meeting of the Bottle Collector's Club was held November 19th at the home of Mr. and Mrs. Lee Scroggin. Several new members were present and added to the roster.

In the informal interim before the meeting was called to order bottles in several rooms were inspected and admired. One table displayed a collection belonging to Darlene and Fred Piggott, who are close neighbors. (The Piggotts have a Dr. Kilmer's Almanac for 1933. It is very interesting. The advertising and pictures were at least 10 years old and show the product to be over 50 years old. My best guess from this is that the great Dr. Kilmer dates back to at least 1873. Fred Ball had a sample bottle of Kilmer's that was full. Whether it was the original product or not, I'm not sure — it smelled of turpentine. — *J. C. T.*)

Finding a name for the club was again brought before the group, and after much discussion a motion was made and seconded that we call ourselves the Antique Bottle Collector's Association of California. The motion carried.

Jackie Scroggin made a motion that Mr. Tibbitts be our president. The motion was seconded and unanimously carried. *F. G. — J. C. T.*

# III
# Advertising Pays
### and
# Culture and Dignity is Added

The regular meeting of ABCAC was held January 21, 1960, at the home of Larry Dunlop and Don Reich. Mr. Tibbitts called the meeting to order. He told us there were 33 new members and also many new associate members since the article in the *Bee* January 3rd. The Tibbitts' phone rang constantly for several days. Mr. and Mrs. Tibbitts recorded all the names and addresses and took notes of interest. There were 17 of these new members present at the meeting and Mr. Tibbitts introduced them.

At this point, Mrs. Grace Neil asked why not start a club scrap book of such pictures and articles of interest. Mr. Tibbitts asked if she would be willing to keep up such a project and said he had some material which could be used. It seems like an excellent idea, and Mrs. Neil has talked herself into a job.

Mr. Blackwell read a letter he had received from the Librarian at Santa Barbara in response to an inquiry he had made about an olive oil bottle. This illustrates the type of information that can be obtained by writing letters and asking questions.

Mr. Tibbitts asked what we thought of starting a catalog list of all our west coast bottles, giving size, shape, color and what is embossed in the glass. This could be worked up first on bitters bottles into a master listing for that group; we could then go on to other classes of bottles. He offered to work up a form and have copies mimeographed to send with the notes of the meeting.

Dave Gwynne inquired if digging is being stopped in the West End Redevelopment area. Don and Larry said the man who is in charge of the work doesn't like holes to be dug and left open, but if you cover up where you have been digging, there is no objection. This should, of course, apply wherever you dig.

Try this on your typewriter instead of the quick brown fox — Pack my box with five dozen liquor jugs. (Contains all letters of the alphabet.)

*F.G.*

Notes from the President:

So — we have added culture and respect to our club by applying and being accepted for membership in the Sacramento Garden and Art Center. We are considered "historical" and are the fourth club in this class. For a sustaining membership of $10.00 per year for the club, we will have a monthly meeting place with kitchen privileges and custodian services. Details at next meeting. Highly approved by members contacted. Only one rub, and this we will have to accept, the only night open is on the first Tuesday. Sorry, and hope it doesn't interfere with too many other meetings.

Tom Brown and Larry Cope have been invited to exhibit at the March 1 meeting. Just friendly kidding — let's call this "The Bitter Battle of the Bitters Bottlers."

*J.C.T.*

## IV
## Inventory of Bitters Bottles Listed
## and
## Some References on Glass and Bottles Given

The March meeting of ABCAC was held at the Sacramento Garden and Arts Center on March 1, 1960. This is a beautiful building and we are fortunate to be a member. The room was set up for 40 odd people and the two displays — 73 people were present. We may get the larger room if we continue to need it.

Bitters inventory produced replies from 23 people, covered 118 bottles, embraced 52 different types. Katherine Ball is setting up a card for each type giving pertinent information. This will be added to as new types are reported to her. She will also add information regarding the product or the bottle as developed by research. If you have any information on Bitters or Bitters Bottles, send it to her and tell her where you found the information.

For the next meeting send in your inventory on Patent Medicine Bottles — Dr. Kilmers, Dr. Kings, Tonics, Sarsaparillas, Balms, Cordials, Elixirs and the like. Sheets included for Associates and Members not at the March 1st meeting.

President reported on article from Geotimes loaned by new member, Eldridge Drew. "Dating of Mining Camps with Tin Cans and Bottles." Tin cans with crimped seams are 1920 and later. Prior to that the seams were soldered. Watch for soldered tin cans. The bottles from the automatic bottle machines showed up in the west about 1920. After this the seams go all the way to the top of the bottle. Prior to this the lip was hand applied and had no seams. Prior to World War I much of the clear glass turned purple.

"Toot" Garten, of Carson City, has discovered a Family Connection of a sort with *Doyles Hop Bitters* (Plate # 2 ). Anyone with duplicate to trade please contact him.

Every member entitled to bring to each meeting, not to exceed, five bottles for trading purposes. Any Associates with duplicates to trade should send in a list.

Any member wanting to show entire collection to groups may post notice at meeting, setting time, place, and number of people who could be handled. Besides two exhibitors each meeting, everyone is requested to bring in any really good find.

On travels carry roster of Members and Associates with you. Look them up.

In the fall we will have a booth at the White Elephant Sale. Monies received are used to operate Center. This will be fun. Clean up and save some bottles to donate to this.

We are the fourth Historical Group in the Center. Feel we would gain much if some of our members would join the Sacramento County Historical Society.

Frank Thornburg's method of checking to see if glass will turn purple. Fill with slaked lime or hold against white paper and hold in sunlight. Look for a pink tinge.

Geotimes article said purple background accelerates turning glass in sun; black or brown retards coloring; others won't help or hurt.

Am listing books, articles, etc., we have found interesting. Note that many were recommended by Members and Associates. Send in any references you know of like these and we will put out a real list of "bottle and glass" reading.

Don Reich had a close call with a cave-in at 2nd and Capitol. Am only mentioning this as a warning. Don't get carried away when digging in excavations or banks. Don got four old "historical" flasks there and Larry Dunlop got one. One of Don's was "Success to the Railroad." Hope they bring them on April 5th.

Another warning: The rattlesnakes are out, so keep your eyes open. Be especially careful around rocks, loose boards, old buildings, etc. Watch those hands and feet! On level ground these boys can only strike one-third their length so it's not too bad — just be careful.

Frank Thornburg's method of cleaning water stain: Vinegar, diced potato, BB shot, and shake. *J.C.T.*

## BOOKS

AMERICAN BOTTLES OLD AND NEW — *Walbridge (Owens)*
MANUFACTURE OF GLASS — *Angus/Butterworth (Composition, Color, Process)*
AMERICAN GLASS — *McKearins (Catalog old bottles)*
BOTTLE AND GLASS HANDBOOK — *D. Maust (E. G. Warman Publ. Co. No. 8, Frankhoover, Union Town, Pa.)*
BOTTLE PRICE GUIDE — *(Same as above)*
TREASURES IN TRUCK AND TRASH — *Morgan Towne (Doubleday & Co., Inc.) Short chapter on glass, but interesting in "sidelines."*
HANDBOOK OF TOMORROW'S ANTIQUES — *Carl W. Dreppard (Thomas Y. Crowell Company) Glass items covered under several categories. Nice photos.*
EARLY AMERICAN GLASS — *Rhea Mansfield Knittle (Garden City Publ. Co.) Glassmaking and early glass houses, nice plates of old glass including some bottles.*

MINE AND MINERAL RESOURCES OF THE COUNTIES OF COLUSA, GLENN, LAKE, MARIN, NAPA, SOLANO AND YOLO *(Report for period 1913-14, California State Printing Office, 1915, California State Mining Bureau.)* To find some soda bottles. It tells who bottled what, and when, and gives locations of bottling works. *Carol Farrell*

THE GOLDEN AGE OF QUACKERY — *Stewart H. Holbrook, 1959. (McMillan Co. $4.95)* One chapter on Asa T. Soule who bought out Doyle's Hop Bitters and became a multi-millionaire in a few years. *T. Garten*

THE OLD COUNTRY STORE — *Gerald Carson (Oxford Press, 1954)* Chapter 11, 1 For A Man, 2 For A Horse. All about old patent medicines. *CF*

MAGIC IN A BOTTLE — *Milt Silverman (New York, 1941)* *Carol Farrell*

THE MIDWEST PIONEER — His Ills, Cures and Doctors — *Madge E. Pickard and R. Carlyle Buley, Crawfordsville, Ind., 1945.* *Carol Farrell*

FOUR WHITE HORSES AND A BRASS BAND — *Violet McNeal, 1941 (Both Doubleday and McClelland)* About medicine shows. *M. L. Blackwell*

## MAGAZINE ARTICLES

FLASKS OF FAME — *True, 12/57, 68-73*

AMERICAN HISTORY IN BOTTLES — *Colliers, 7/15/50, 50*

THESE ARE REAL CHARACTERS — *American Home, 5/56*

DATING OF MINING CAMPS WITH TIN CANS AND BOTTLES — *Chas. B. Hunt, Geotimes, May-June 1959, American Geological Inst. E. Drew*

OLD TIME REMEDIES — *Lula Walker, Rural New Yorker, 1/7/50, 100th Anniversary Issue. Carol Farrell*

THE MEDICINE SHOW — *American Mercury, 6/25.* If you have "Nonpariel Rubbing Oil" or "Tono Tonic" you should own this. Interesting article anyway.

## ALMANACS

DR. KILMERS — *Year 1933. Piggotts have a copy.*

DR. HOSTETTERS — *Year 1861. Tibbitts have a copy.*

Hostetter started in 1853. In 1859 they shipped 7000 dozen bottles to California. Must have been good stuff.

Questionnaire No. 1 — March 1, 1960
BITTERS BOTTLES
(Only those with the word *Bitters* in the glass)

1 — African Stomach Bitters
1 — Atwood's Jannace or Jannaice Bitters
1 — Atwood's Jaundice Bitters
1 — Ayer's Bitters
1 — Baker's Orange Grove Bitters
1 — Clarke's Vegetable Sherry Wine Bitters (½ gallon)
1 — Caldewell's Herb Bitters (The Great Tonic)
1 — Climax Bitters
2 — Damiana Bitters
2 — Doyle's Hop Bitters
1 — Electric Bitters
2 — Electric Brand Bitters
1 — Ferro-Quina Bitters
1 — Greeley's Bourbon Bitters
1 — Halls Bitters
1 — Dr. Harter's Wild Cherry Bitters

4 – Dr. Harter's Wild Cherry Bitters, St. Louis
 1 – Dr. Henley's Wild Grape Root Bitters IXL
 1 – Dr. Henley's Wild Grape Root Bitters (IXL)
 1 – Dr. Hoofland's German Bitters
12 – Dr. J. Hostetter's Bitters
 1 – Iron Bitters
 1 – Dr. Jacob's Bitters
 1 – Kimball's Jaundice Bitters
 1 – Lacour's Bitters
 1 – Lash's Bitters (with screwtop neck)
 1 – Sample Lash's Bitters (miniature)
 4 – Lash's Bitters Co., New York, Chicago, San Francisco
 1 – Lash's Bitters Co., San Francisco
11 – Lash's Kidney and Liver Bitters
 1 – Lash's Liver Bitters
 3 – Lediard's Celebrated Stomach Bitters
 2 – E. Dexter Loveridge Wahoo Bitters
 3 – Marshall's Bitters
 1 – Mohica Bitters
 1 – Morning Bitters Inceptum
 1 – Old Sachem Bitters and Wigwam Tonic
 3 – Peruvian Bitters
 1 – Phoenix Bitters
 1 – S. O. Richardson's Bitters
 1 – Dr. C. W. Roback's Stomack Bitters Cinncinati, Ohio
 1 – Romany Wine Bitters
 1 – Royal Italian Bitters
 1 – Schroeder's Bitters
 1 – W. F. Severa Stomack Bitters
 1 – Dr. A. H. Smith's Old Style Bitters
 1 – Star Kidney and Liver Bitters
 1 – Alex Van Humboldt's Bitters
 1 – Wahoo and Calisaya Bitters
 4 – Wait's Kidney and Liver Bitters
 5 – J. Walker's V.B. (Vinegar Bitters: 2 aqua, 1 deep aqua,
         1 chartreuse and 1 green)

Total members reporting:              21
Number of bottles:                   116
(Including duplicates of brand names and variants)
Number of brand names:                45
Most Frequent:
    Hostetters    12        Drake's       5
    Yerba Buena    7        J. Walker's   5

## V
### First Field Trip Discussed... Club Continues to Grow...
### Dear Lydia...

On Tuesday, April 5, 1960, the regular meeting of the ABCAC was held at the Garden and Arts Center. This month we had a larger room, which was set up to accommodate 80 people and we believe every seat was filled. In fact, we heard later about a couple who came a little late, saw no place to sit, and didn't come in. Always come in — we can get more chairs.

Beautiful bottles were on display, thanks to Frank Thornburg and also Mr. Sturgill from the "Mother Lode Bottle Bonanza" in Auburn. In this collection were many labeled bottles which must have been pushed back on a shelf somewhere and forgotten. Another table held some beautiful purple bottles presented to Tom Brown by Mr. Harris of Sacramento who picked them up in Nevada twenty years ago. Most outstanding in Mr. Thornburg's collection was a Virginia Dare turned purple and a beautiful blue quart bottle.

Ed Hughes, a member who had been unable to attend meetings before, was introduced and gave us some interesting information on his correspondence and collaboration with the author of a new book being written in the east on bitters bottles. This book will be much larger than its predecessor, "Early American Bottles and Flasks," with many illustrations and actual photographs. The author is Bart Saalfrank and the book is dedicated to Charles Gardner. It will be out this fall.

Frank Thornburg showed some of his bottles and gave us one of his recipes for cleaning. This consists of pumice stone, BB shot, and "gunk." Gunk is a cleaner used in garages, etc., costs 89¢ a can and Frank claims is very effective if you can stand the smell. With this mixture, of course, goes lots of shaking.

Mr. Tibbitts suggested the weekend of July 9-10 as a tentative date for a group field trip to Masonic. This is a complete ghost town with absolutely no facilities nor inhabitants. However, a motel can be reached in a 45-minute drive each way if you do not wish to camp out. There is a running stream. The altitude is around 7000 feet so it will be cold at night. Sounds like fun whether we find any bottles or not. Quite a few members showed interest in such a trip and Mr. Tibbitts asked those planning to go to sign a slip on the table. More about this excursion will be discussed later. Any other members or associates interested should advise Mr. Tibbitts. Masonic is near Bridgeport.

This group started last October with a letter addressed to five people. We now have 47 local families, or 74 individuals; 40 out-of-town families, or 59 individuals. A total of 87 families or 133 individual members. Mr. Tibbitts still receives several letters of inquiry every week.

Mrs. Osborne of Redding wrote that: (1) The Desert Magazine for October, 1959, has a very nice article on coloring of glass — why it turns, etc. (2) She uses a mixture of vinegar, detergent and parakeet gravel for cleaning. Mr. Hopkins gave us some interesting facts about early Sacramento history and Doggin's Drug Store, at 262 J Street.

Mr. Harris told us of working over twenty years in Nevada at the mining camp of Fairview on the old Pony Express Route north of Highway 50. He picked up old original wood insulators and 500 feet of the first telegraph line from St. Joseph, Missouri, to Sacramento. Most of these things have been placed in museums in various parts of the country. The bottles he gave Tom Brown are a beautiful deep purple.

Sorry Don and Larry missed the meeting. We would like to see those flasks and hear about the gold piece!

Bea Boynton of Quincy reports a preliminary bottle club meeting inter-

PLATE 1. Left to right. BITTERS.

- 9" high, square, amber, BIMAL.
  F – LASH'S KIDNEY AND LIVER BITTERS
  B – THE BEST CATHARTIC AND BLOOD PURIFIER

- 6-5/8" high, rect. w/beveled corners, aqua, BIMALOP.
  F – S. O. RICHARDSON'S
  L – BITTERS
  B – SOUTH READING
  R – MASS.

- 12½" high, triangular, amber, BIMALGP.
  F – MORNING * BITTERS  (vertical)
      INCEPTUM 5869  (horizontal)
  R – PATENTED 5869

- 12¼" high, Ear of corn, amber, BIMAL.
  F – NATIONAL BITTERS
  Bm – PATENT 1867

PLATE 2. Left to right. BITTERS.

- 9¾" high, square, semi tall cabin, amber, BIMAL.
  F – <u>1872</u>  (hop vine stem w/4 leaves, 2 blossoms)
  L – <u>BITTERS</u>
  R – <u>DOYLES</u>
  B – <u>HOP</u>

- 10" high, square, tall cabin, amber, BIMAL. 4 log.
  F – <u>ST DRAKES 1860 PLANTATION X BITTERS</u>
  B – <u>PATENTED 1862</u>

- 6¼" high, 12 sided, aqua, BIMAL.
  1 – <u>ATWOOD'S</u>
  2 – <u>JAUNDICE BITTERS</u>
  3 – <u>M. CARTER & SON</u>
  4 – <u>GEORGETOWN</u>
  5 – <u>MASS.</u>

- 12" high, round, aqua, BIMAL.
  F – <u>DAMIANA BITTERS</u>
  B – <u>BAJA CALIFORNIA</u>
  * – <u>LEWIS HESS MANUF'R</u>   *(around shoulder)

ested many people. Let us know if we can help you up there.
Next Meeting Exhibitors: Ed Hughes — Bitters and ? ? ?
The Tibbitts — "Purple" and ? ? ?

The Tibbitts will also bring a bottle bottom and a bottle neck recovered from the sea, last year, off Port Royal, Jamaica. These fragments had been in the sea since June 7, 1692. They were recovered by the Geographic-Smithsonian-Link Expedition as reported in the very interesting article in the February 1960 National Geographic.

Another interesting book: "*Lydia Pinkham* (Plate # 4 ) Is Her Name," by Jean Burton, Farrar Straus and Company.

*Let us sing of Lydia Pinkham*
*And her love of the Human Race*
*How she sells her Vegetable Compound*
*And the papers copied her face.*

*There's a baby in every bottle*
*So the old quotation ran*
*But the Federal Trade Commission*
*Still insists you'll need a man.*

F.G. & J.C.T.

# VI
# Resume of Patent Medicine Inventory
# and
# Historical Flasks & Gold Coin
# Dug in Sacramento

The regular meeting of the ABCAC was held Tuesday, May 3rd, at the Sacramento Garden and Arts Center. Bottles were on display from the collections of the Ed Hughes and the John Tibbitts families.

Mr. Tibbitts talked about our field trip to Masonic on July 9th and 10th. This is not a complete town — just a few buildings are left standing. Bottle hunting may be much better other places, but you can't always camp out where the digging is good. Plans are to meet in front of the courthouse in Bridgeport at 9-9:30 Saturday morning (this means leaving Sacramento about 5 a.m.), have a second breakfast, and leave for Masonic at 10 a.m. sharp. To reach Bridgeport, you drive on Highway 50 to just across the state line and turn right on Kingsbury Grade to Highway 395 and then south to Bridgeport. From Bridgeport to Masonic is approximately 13 miles. Those planning to stay at a motel in Bridgeport should make reservations early. There are at least four motels, the East Walker, Slick's and two others. Campers and picnickers should plan to bring all food and water. There is a dishwashing stream only. Suggestions for the meals in camp: Saturday's lunch should be something cold already prepared. For Saturday night dinner, everyone could have steaks (if you like steak) to cook on a grill. Sunday morning breakfast, probably bacon and eggs, and Sunday's lunch again something cold or easily prepared, so there is plenty of time for exploration and digging. A warning — don't bring any house trailers — the hills are too steep.

Mr. Tibbitts thanked Ed Hughes for his nice display of Bitters bottles, old iron toys and banks. This was only a small portion of his fine collection. Ed reported that Mr. Saalfrank, who is writing the new book on bitters bottles has been quite ill and may not be able to finish the book as planned. The Craigs of Sparks will be given credit in the book for their Hira Picara Extract of Figs.

Mr. Tibbitts also thanked Larry and Don for coming and showing the historical flasks they found in the West End. Don described how they were found about seven feet underground where an oil company was excavating for a service station at 2nd and Capitol. They are clean and like new which proves all old bottles are not dirty. Don said there must have been 30 or more all together in a group. These flasks date back to 1835-45 and were made by the Keen Glass Works in New Jersey. There is only one other flask of this group that they do not have. They also found a $3 gold coin which they sold to a collector for $75. This was found next to the Lincoln Theatre at 3rd and L.

Questionnaire No. 2 – MEDICINE BOTTLES

Total number of reports . . . . . . . . . . . . . . . . 24
Total number bottles listed. . . . . . . . . . . . . 530
Trade names . . . . . . . . . . . . . . . . . . . . . . . 257
Types:
   With Doctor as part of trade name . . . . . . . . . 52
   Druggists and Pharmacists only . . . . . . . . . .  9
   Companies and Laboratories only . . . . . . . . . 11
   Prescription bottles . . . . . . . . . . . . . . . . .  3
   Cosmetics . . . . . . . . . . . . . . . . . . . . . . . .  8
   Poison . . . . . . . . . . . . . . . . . . . . . . . . . .  1
   Proprietary medicines . . . . . . . . . . . . . . . 156
   To be classified . . . . . . . . . . . . . . . . . . . 17
Most frequent:
   Davis Vegetable Pain Killer . . . . . . . . . . . . 14
   Scott's Emulsion . . . . . . . . . . . . . . . . . . . 14
   Dr. D. Jayne's Tonic Vermifuge . . . . . . . . . . 12
   Vaseline . . . . . . . . . . . . . . . . . . . . . . . . .  9
   Citrate of Magnesia . . . . . . . . . . . . . . . . .  8
   Hamlin's Wizard Oil . . . . . . . . . . . . . . . . .  8
   Lydia E. Pinkham's Vegetable Compound. . . .  8
   Warner's Safe Kidney and Liver Cure . . . . . .  8

One of our neophyte bottle collectors had a sad experience recently. In his absence, his wife asked her father to carry out the trash on the back porch, and guess what the father-in-law included in the trash? Oh well, you can always start over.                                  F.G. & J.C.T.

# VII
## Invited to Display at Shows
## and
## Research Information

The June meeting of the ABCAC was held at the Sacramento Garden and Arts Center on Tuesday, June 7.

Mr. Lester, Display Chairman for Sacramento Mineral Society, said they would be very happy to have the Bottle Club fill a couple of display cases in their exhibit at the County Fair June 16, 17, 18, and 19. Mr. Tibbitts, Mr. Ross and Barbara Keskeys volunteered to meet at the Fairgrounds on Wednesday evening, June 15, and arrange an exhibit.

Frank Thornberg also suggested we have a display at Folsom this fall at the combined Art Show (depicting historical scenes), display of antique firearms, and old Firemen's uniforms. (Let's put in some thought on putting on a good show of our own sometime. Your president has discussed this with Mrs. Shepard, President of the Sacramento Garden & Arts Center, and she would like very much to have us do it.

Mrs. Sheehan advises that Roth & Co. was not listed in the San Francisco Directory after 1888. She is going to send us more information on Roth & Co., also Dr. Pierce, Foley & Co., Warners, and others. Thanks, Mrs. Sheehan. If more of you would do this, our researchers would sure appreciate it and we would get to our goal sooner.

Marian Jewett reports a product that she has tried which removes alkali stains etc. from bottles — "Lymoff," Lymoff Co., 1674 Juliet St., St. Paul 15, Minn.

Your president just found two interesting advertising pamphlets — "Lifesavers," Miles Medical Co., Elkhart, Ind.; "Pierce's Memorandum Account Book." Dr. Miles advertises his Restorative Nervine, New Heart Cure, Anti-Pain Pills, Blood Purifier, Restorative Tonic, Nerve & Liver Pills, Nerve Plasters. Dr. Pierce advertises his "Golden Medical Discovery," Pleasant Purgative Pellets, Favorite Prescription, Dr. Sage's Catarrh Remedy, Compound Extract of Smart Weed and "The People's Common Sense Medical Adviser."

Does anyone have any of Dr. Root's medicine bottles? I have his book "The People's Medical Lighthouse," 10th Edition, 1854. In the back, this book advertises "Dr. H. K. Root's Sixteen Vegetable Blood Remedies." — Blood Renovator, Anti-Bilious Pills, Heart Regulator, Lung Corrector, German Ointment, Catarrh Snuff, Cancer Eradicator, Female Wash, Water Regulator, Hair Producer, Eye Water, Ear Lotion, Worm Killer, Inhaling Fluid, Dysentery Specific, Nervine, and Elixir of Life. (I count 17). Most of these were 50¢ and $1.00 per bottle, but the Elixir ("For use in cases of Nervous Debility, loss of Nervous Electric and Procreating Energy, etc., etc.") was $3.00 per bottle. (And would have been worth it if it could do all that was claimed). His Worm Killer was "For destroying the life of and expelling from the human system Tape Worms, Round Worms, Thread Worms, Pin Worms, Evets, Frogs, Snakes, and every living thing of whatever kind, that may be existing in the stomach or bowels." (Anyone swallowed a snake lately?) This book is small print and has 470 pages. It was owned by Dr. John C. Taylor, so must have been used by the doctors of the time. *F.G. & J.C.T.*

## VIII
## Complete Listing of Patent Medicine Inventory

Notes from September 6, 1960 Meeting and other items . . .

Not many at September meeting which was my fault — no notes, no notice, no nothing. Summer is a bad time. Real good meeting accidentally. Everyone brought their summer finds which were most interesting. Jody Lewis brought the bronze Masonic commemorative plaque he found on the Masonic field trip among other things. The Thompsons, the Winters, the Browns, and yours truly brought bottles. Thanks so much.

Have received some good research information from some of you associates. Notes are too long to include now but maybe we can put out a yearly "What We Have Learned to Date" and send it out to all. This would entail quite a bit of work — anyone interested?

Mr. Saalfrank is quite ill and may not complete his book on Bitters. We are very sorry to hear this.

The Masonic field trip saw quite a little group of "bottlers" in the old deserted town. Not too many real good finds were made but everyone got a few to bring home. Present were:

| | |
|---|---|
| Bea Boynton and friend | Quincy |
| "Toot" & Dorothy Garten | Carson City |
| Phillip & Kathrine Kratz | China Lake |
| Joe, Virginia & Jody Lewis | Broderick |
| George & Harriet Reiber | Sacramento |
| Lee & Jackie Scroggin | Sacramento |
| and the Tibbitts | |

I'm including a simple listing of our medicine bottle inventory as received. Prize for the biggest bottle contribution here goes to Toot and Dorothy Garten. A lot of thanks to Katherine Ball for getting this together and to the typists who put the information on cards for us — Jackie Scroggin and Dorothy Brown.

A. C. Revi, Art Glass Studio, P.O. Box 7292, Dallas, Texas, would like to hear from any of you "on your collections of figure bottles — hands, animals, people — especially." Wants material for series of articles now running each month in Hobbies magazine.

Don Reich knows someone in the East who is writing a book, "Wine, Women, and Bottles," to be published in New York in 1962. He may contact our members for information. More power to him.

Thanks to Jackie Scroggin for typing up these notes. We spent a pleasant Saturday afternoon together cussin' our respective typewriters. A little room here so will include a quote from my Pierce's Memorandum Account Book, 1885-1886. "Dr. Pierce's Compound Extract of SMART WEED or Water Pepper. Compounded of Smart-Weed, Jamaica Ginger, Anodyne and Healing Gums, and the BEST FRENCH BRANDY — Taken internally it cures Diarrhoea, Dysentery (Bloody-flux), Summer Complaint, Cholera, Cholera Morbus, Cholera Infantum, Colic, Cramps and Pain in the Stomach; breaks up Colds, Febrile and Inflammatory Attacks, Rheumatism, and Neuralgia, and relieves all Pains and Suppressions to which Females are subject from taking cold at a critical period. Applied Externally it Cures Sprains and Bruises, Frost-bites, Chilblains, Rheumatic Affections, Neuralgia, Pain in the Back, Soreness and Stiffness of Joints, Stings and Bites of Poisonous Insects and Reptiles, Caked Breasts, or "Ague in Breast" and enlarged glands — in short, is an unexcelled Liniment for Man and Beast. Price 50 cents by Druggists. World's Dispensary Medical Association, Prop'rs. 630 Main Street, Buffalo, N.Y." So there! Wonder who they were calling a beast, not man.

We picked up three more Almanacs this summer:

92ND YEAR OF DR. J.H. MC LEAN'S MEDICAL ALMANAC, *1945;*
SWAMP ROOT DREAM BOOK & ALMANAC, *Dr. Kilmer, 1935 (advertises more than 50 years of reputation);*
RAWLEIGHS 1917 ALMANAC, *28th year.* 140 Products including 31 medicines. *J.C.T.*

Simple list of Medicine Bottles as reported on Questionnaire #2. Some spelling variations have been combined. Number of different people reporting the same bottle also shown. Only a relatively few members and associates reported. If you enjoy this type of info why not help out and report next time?

### THOSE WITH DR. OR DOCTOR AS PART OF THE TRADE NAME

Dr. Ira Baker's Cough Balsam . . . . . . . . . . . . . . . . . . . . . . . . . . . 1
Dr. Bell's Pine Tar Honey . . . . . . . . . . . . . . . . . . . . . . . . . . . . . 1
Dr. A. Bochee's German Syrup . . . . . . . . . . . . . . . . . . . . . . . . . 4
Dr. Buchard's Auroline . . . . . . . . . . . . . . . . . . . . . . . . . . . . . . . 1
Dr. J.W. Bull's Cough Syrup . . . . . . . . . . . . . . . . . . . . . . . . . . . 1
Dr. E.C. Balm . . . . . . . . . . . . . . . . . . . . . . . . . . . . . . . . . . . . . . 1
Dr. W.B. Caldwell's Syrup Pepsin . . . . . . . . . . . . . . . . . . . . . . . 3
Dr. W.B. Caldwell's . . . . . . . . . . . . . . . . . . . . . . . . . . . . . . . . . 2
Dr. Cummings Vegetine . . . . . . . . . . . . . . . . . . . . . . . . . . . . . . 1
Dr. Peter Fahrneys & Sons Co. . . . . . . . . . . . . . . . . . . . . . . . . . 2
   (see The Reliable Old Time Preparation)
Dr. T.W. Graydon . . . . . . . . . . . . . . . . . . . . . . . . . . . . . . . . . . . 1
Dr. Henley's Celery, Beef and Iron . . . . . . . . . . . . . . . . . . . . . . 2
Dr. D. Jayne & Co. . . . . . . . . . . . . . . . . . . . . . . . . . . . . . . . . . . 2
Dr. D. Jayne's Carminative Balsam . . . . . . . . . . . . . . . . . . . . . 2
Dr. D. Jayne's Expectorant. . . . . . . . . . . . . . . . . . . . . . . . . . . . 7
Dr. D. Jayne's Tonic Vermifuge. . . . . . . . . . . . . . . . . . . . . . . . . 8
Dr. D. Jayne's Tonic Vermifuge The Strength Giver . . . . . . . . . . . . . 4
Dr. Kilmer Swamp Root . . . . . . . . . . . . . . . . . . . . . . . . . . . . . . 1
Dr. Kilmer's Swamp Root Kidney Liver and Bladder Cure. . . . . . . . . . 7
Sample Bottle Dr. Kilmer's Swamp Root Kidney Cure . . . . . . . . . . . 2
The Great Dr. Kilmer's Swamp Root Kidney & Bladder Cure Specific . . 1
The Great Dr. Kilmer's Swamp Root Kidney Liver & Bladder
   Cure Specific . . . . . . . . . . . . . . . . . . . . . . . . . . . . . . . . . . . 2
The Great Dr. Kilmer's Swamp Root Kidney Liver & Bladder Remedy. . 2
Dr. King's New Discovery for Constipation . . . . . . . . . . . . . . . . . 1
Dr. King's New Discovery for Consumption . . . . . . . . . . . . . . . . 7
Dr. King's New Discovery for Coughs and Colds . . . . . . . . . . . . . . 4
Dr. August Koenig's Hamburger Tropfen . . . . . . . . . . . . . . . . . . . 1
Dr. D. Kennedy's Favorite Remedy. . . . . . . . . . . . . . . . . . . . . . . 1
Dr. Kennedy's Medical Discovery. . . . . . . . . . . . . . . . . . . . . . . . 1
Dr. J.J. McBride King of Pain . . . . . . . . . . . . . . . . . . . . . . . . . . 1
Dr. J.H. McLean's Volcanic Oil Linament . . . . . . . . . . . . . . . . . . 4
Dr. J.H. McLean's Liver and Kidney Balm . . . . . . . . . . . . . . . . . 1
Doc Marshall's Catarrh Snuff. . . . . . . . . . . . . . . . . . . . . . . . . . . 1
Dr. Mile's Heart Treatment . . . . . . . . . . . . . . . . . . . . . . . . . . . . 3
Dr. Mile's Medicine Co. . . . . . . . . . . . . . . . . . . . . . . . . . . . . . . 1
Dr. Miles Nervine . . . . . . . . . . . . . . . . . . . . . . . . . . . . . . . . . . . 1
Dr. Mile's Restorative Nervine . . . . . . . . . . . . . . . . . . . . . . . . . 3
Dr. Mile's Restorative Blood Purifier . . . . . . . . . . . . . . . . . . . . . 1
Dr. Nunn's Black Oil Healing Compound . . . . . . . . . . . . . . . . . . 3
Dr. Peters Kuriko . . . . . . . . . . . . . . . . . . . . . . . . . . . . . . . . . . . 1

Dr. Peter's Oleoid .................................. 1
Dr. Peter's Oleum .................................. 1
Dr. Peter's Vigor .................................. 1
R.V. Pierce, M.D. (see Extract of Smart Weed)
Dr. Pierce's Favorite Prescription ........................ 6
Dr. Pierce's Golden Medical Discovery ..................... 4
Dr. S. Pitcher's Castoria .............................. 6
Dr. Sage's Catarrh Remedy ............................ 1
Dr. Shoop's Family Medicines .......................... 1
Dr. Thompson's Eye Water ............................ 5
Dr. True's Elixir .................................... 1
Nathan Tucker, M.D. Specific for Asthma, Hay Fever, and all
 Diseases of the Respiratory Organs ..................... 1
Dr. Wistar's Balsam of Wild Cherry ....................... 2
Dr. Wood's Liver Regulator ............................ 2
(End of Doctors Section)

| | |
|---|---|
| Absorbine Jr. | 2 |
| Aker's English Remedy for the Throat and Lungs | 2 |
| The Allanbury's Castor Oil | 1 |
| Armour and Co. Digestive Ferments | 1 |
| Athlophoros | 1 |
| Ayer's Cherry Pectoral | 8 |
| Ayer's Sarsaparilla | 2 |
| Ayer's Sarsaparilla Compound Extract | 4 |
| Ayer's Pills | 5 |
| B & S Homeopathic Cough and Croup Syrup | 1 |
| Balsam of Honey | 1 |
| Barry's Tricopherous | 1 |
| Bell-Ans | 1 |
| Betul-Ol for External Use | 1 |
| Bliss Liver and Kidney Cure | 1 |
| Bromo Seltzer | 2 |
| F. Brown's Ess of Jamaica Ginger | 2 |
| Buffalo Lithis Water Natures Materia Medica | 1 |
| Burnett's Cocaine | 3 |
| C.C.C. Tonic | 1 |
| Caldwell's Syrup Pepsin | 2 |
| California Fig Syrup Co. | 1 |
| California Fig Syrup Co. Wheeling W. Va. | 2 |
| California Fig Syrup Co. Louisville, Kentucky San Francisco Cal. | 1 |
| Calif. Fig Syrup Co. Califig Sterling Products Inc. Successor | 5 |
| Campe's California Cherry Cordial | 1 |
| Chas. H. Fletcher's Castoria | 6 |
| Chamberlain's Colic Cholera & Diarrhea Remedy | 4 |
| Chamberlain's Cough Remedy | 7 |
| Chamberlain's Pain Balm | 3 |
| Citrate of Magnesia | 7 |
| J.E. Combaults Caustic Balm | 1 |

| | |
|---|---|
| Constitution Water | 1 |
| Cooper's New Discovery | 2 |
| The Cuticura System of Curing Constitutional Humors | 1 |
| Cuticura System of Blood and Skin Purification | 1 |
| Davis Vegetable Painkiller | 14 |
| D.D.D. | 2 |
| Dodson's Liver-Tone | 3 |
| The Duffy Malt Whiskey Company | 3 |
| Ely's Cream Balm | 3 |
| Eno's Fruit Salt Derivative Compound | 1 |
| Espey's Fragrant Cream | 1 |
| Extract of Smart Weed | 1 |
| Extract Valerian Shaker Fluid | 1 |
| Fellow's Syrup of Hypophosphites | 3 |
| Floroplexion Despepsia Liver Complaint & Consumption | 1 |
| Foley's Kidney Cure | 1 |
| Foley's Kidney & Bladder Cure | 1 |
| Foley's Pain Killer | 1 |
| Forni's Magenstarcker | 1 |
| Forny's Alpenkrauter Blutbeleber *(Hope this translates clean)* | 1 |
| Foscates Anodyne Cordial | 1 |
| Fruitola Pinus Medicine Co. | 1 |
| Gauss Elixir | 1 |
| Glover's Imperial Mange Remedy | 1 |
| Glover's Imperial Mange Remedy 6½ Fl. Oz. | 2 |
| Golden's Liquid Beef Tonic | 1 |
| J.E. Gombault's Caustic Balm | 1 |
| Glyco-Thymoline | 3 |
| Groves Tastless Chill Tonic | 2 |
| Hales Honey of Horehound and Tar | 1 |
| Hall's Balsam for the Lungs | 3 |
| Hall's Catarrh Cure | 4 |
| Hall's Catarrh Medicine | 1 |
| Hall's Pulmonary Balsam | 1 |
| Hall's Sarsaparilla | 1 |
| Hamlin's Wizard Oil | 8 |
| Valentine Hasswer's Lung & Cough Syrup | 1 |
| Hay's Hair Health | 1 |
| Henry's Calcined Magnesia | 1 |
| H.H.H. Horse Medicine D.D.T. 1868 | 1 |
| H.H.H. The Celebrated Horse Medicine D.D.T. 1868 | 1 |
| Himalaya The Kola Compound Nature's Cure for Asthma | 1 |
| Hood's Compound Extract Sarsaparilla | 3 |
| Hood's Pills Cure Liver Ills | 3 |
| Hood's Sarsaparilla | 4 |
| Hood's Sarsaparilla Apothecaries | 2 |
| Hopp's Linament | 1 |

| | |
|---|---|
| Husband's Calcined Magnesia | 4 |
| India Cholacoque | 1 |
| Indian Sagwa | 1 |
| Injection Brow | 2 |
| Jaffe's Electric Pain Expeller | 1 |
| Jongaline | 1 |
| Joy's Sarsaparilla | 2 |
| Kickapoo Indian Cough Cure | 1 |
| Kutnow's Powder | 1 |
| Lash's Products Co. | 1 |
| Laxol | 4 |
| Liquozone | 1 |
| Listerine | 2 |
| Lozogo del Dr. Pietro | 1 |
| The Maltine Mfg. Co. | 1 |
| McLean's Volcanic Oil Linament | 1 |
| McMillan & Kester's Ess of Jamaica Ginger S.F. | 1 |
| MAC for Despepsia & Constipation | 1 |
| Mayr's Wonderful Remedy | 2 |
| Medicated Aerated Waters | 1 |
| Mexican Mustang Liniment | 3 |
| Milk's Emulsion | 1 |
| Moone's Emerald Oil | 1 |
| The Mother's Friend | 6 |
| The Mother's Helper | 1 |
| Munn's Elixir of Opium | 1 |
| Murine Eye Remedy Co. | 5 |
| Newbro's Herpicide for the Scalp | 1 |
| Olive Tar | 1 |
| Omega Oil It's Green | 1 |
| Optimus | 1 |
| Osgood's India Chilagogue | 1 |
| Pain Expeller for Muscular Aches and Pains | 1 |
| Paine's Celery Compound | 5 |
| Parker's Ginger Tonic | 1 |
| Parto Glory for the Nerves | 1 |
| Pepto-dangan "Gude" | 2 |
| Pesco's Cure for Consumption | 1 |
| 30 Phenolax Wafers | 1 |
| Phillip's Milk of Magnesia | 2 |
| Pinex | 1 |
| Lydia Pinkham's Blood Purifier | 1 |
| Lydia E. Pinkham's Medicine | 3 |
| Lydia E. Pinkham's Vegetable Compound | 8 |
| The Piso Company | 1 |
| Piso's Cure | 1 |
| Piso's Cure for Consumption | 2 |
| Pratt's Abolition Oil for Consumption | 1 |
| Psychine | 1 |
| Prof. Callan's World Renowned Brazillian Gum | 1 |
| Prof. Decrath's Electric Oil | 1 |

| | |
|---|---|
| Redington & Co. Ess. of Jamaica Ginger, San Francisco | 2 |
| The Reliable Old Time Preparation | 3 |
| Riker's Expectorant | 1 |
| Riker's Compound Sarsaparilla | 1 |
| Rionharts FLAXSEED Balsom | 1 |
| St. Jakob's Oil | 2 |
| Sanford's Jamaica Ginger | 1 |
| Sands Sarsaparilla | 1 |
| Save-the-Horse Spavin Cure | 1 |
| Schenck's Pulmonic Syrup | 1 |
| Scott's Emulsion | 14 |
| Tillman's Oil | 1 |
| G. de Koning Tilly | 1 |
| Sedlitz C H Chanteaud Sordes Francs Burgeous Paris | 1 |
| Shiloh Cure | 1 |
| Shiloh's Consumption Cure | 3 |
| Simmons Liver Regulator | 1 |
| Sloans Liniment | 3 |
| Sloan's Liniment Kills Pain 3 oz. | 2 |
| Slocum's Coltsfoot Expectorant | 1 |
| Smith's Bile Beans | 3 |
| Somnos | 1 |
| Suffolk Harlem Oil | 1 |
| Syrup of Figs | 3 |
| Syrup of Hypohosphites | 1 |
| Trommer Extract of Malt Co. | 1 |
| Vapo Cresolene Co. | 3 |
| Vaseline | 10 |
| Vitaline | 2 |
| Wait's Wild Cherry Tonic, the Great Tonic | 3 |
| Warner's Safe Kidney & Liver Cure | 7 |
| Warner's Safe Nervine | 1 |
| Warner's Safe Rheumatic Cure | 2 |
| Watkins Dandruff Remover & Scalp Tonic | 1 |
| Web's A No. 1 Cathartic Tonic | 3 |
| Wine of Cardin McElree's | 1 |
| Mrs. Winslow's Soothing Syrup | 6 |
| Wulfing's Formamint | 1 |
| Wynkoop's Iceland Pectoral | 3 |

## IX
## More Shows and More Research

The regular meeting of ABCAC was held at Sacramento Garden and Arts Center on Tuesday, Oct. 4th.

More about the plaque Jody Lewis found on the field trip to Masonic this summer. He found it in a covered can. It commemorates the dedication of the House of the Temple (Scottish Rite, Southern Section) finished in 1915; each person attending was given one of the plaques, and a few were sent out. Jody also gave us an interesting account of a trip they took this summer to Moore's Flats, a ghost town. (Ed Hughes advises staying away from that territory, however, until deer season is over; a bottle digger might look like he had horns).

The Sacramento Mineral Society will have a show November 5th and 6th and they will have at least two cases available for us to exhibit bottles again. They would like particularly to have Don Reich's historic flasks on exhibit. They found people much interested in the bottles shown at the June County Fair.

Edith Tibbitts also told us the first Saturday and Sunday in February are set for our Bottle Show. There will be other displays from the other historical groups.

Frank Thornberg and Ed Hughes put on a display of bottles the day of the Pony Express Run in Folsom.

Mr. Rieber told about visiting associate member May Jones in Bishop. He said she has a very attractive home and has bottles all over the house and yard — anyone passing through Bishop should call on her. Mr. Tibbitts has had several letters from her also.

Mrs. Handy of Marysville told us about her brother (who has a store in Forest Hill called Mac's TV & Appliance) who turns bottles purple in four weeks. His "contraption" is a butcher light in a metal box lined with foil. Small bottles, especially flasks, put in this container with the lamp in the bottom, turn a deep purple in approximately four weeks.

(Apologies from your Secretary who goofed off and didn't get any notes out on the August meeting. Mr. Huson conducted an interesting informal meeting in Mr. Tibbitts' absence which we all enjoyed. Sorry I didn't follow through. I really was sick, though, when Mr. T. put out the September report. A bit of wisdom from Mr. Huson — remember old timers never carried their junk uphill, so look in ravines where it could have been dumped downhill. Also, he has a Pacific Coast Public Directory of 1876, which has all business people of western states listed. He won't loan it, but will look up information for you. — *F.G.*)

ODDS AND ENDS — *J.C.T.*

Wonder if that "which" in the last paragraph refers to my absence or Mr. Huson's meeting?

A friend of Tom and Grace Neil, Jim Salling, wrote this little ditty about them:

### *ANY RAGS, BOTTLES, SACKS?*

*You'll find them every week end*
*Digging in some dump*
*Looking for old bottles*
*Most of us call junk.*

*They have a little hoe and rake*
*And dig around like gophers*
*They just can't wait till the work week ends*
*You can see they are not loafers.*

*Now, Grace first got the bug*
*Then Tom got in the act*
*Their house is full of bottles*
*And that my boy's a fact.*

*There are short ones and tall ones*
*Stacked from roof to floor*
*They'll have to move out in the yard*
*To make space for more.*

*Now bottles are containers*
*As are bags and cans*
*They are made for liquids*
*And also specimens.*

*Now I also like bottles*
*They don't need be old*
*Just as long as they are full*
*To warm me when I'm cold.*

We have been asked by Mr. Jewel, archeologist at American River J.C. to help one of his students. This student, Sammy Payen, has been active in the archeological work in connection with the excavation at Sutter's Fort. He wants us to help date the findings by attempting to date the bottles and fragments that were excavated. Am meeting with him at the Fort on Saturday afternoon, October 29, and will welcome some help.

Here is a (translation from Dutch) letter sent us by Mary Ford, Bishop, on the *Hoboken* (Plate # 9 ) bottles. Note the Fremery reference if you have a Fremery whiskey.

"The bottle with the label 'A van Hoboken' comes from our subsidiary company, the Hoboken de Bie & Co. distillers, established at Rotterdam, although this one is a separate partnership under separate company. We are very close to that company, because both companies have some of the same partners.

"The company Hoboken de Bie & Co. started in 1790 as a subsidiary company by the A van Hoboken Co. established by Anthony van Hoboken in 1774, in 1848 changed into the A. van Hoboken & Co. The partners now are J.H. van Hoboken, J.H. van Hoboken Jr., and H. van Hoboken.

"The work at the Hoboken de Bie Co. includes the distilling of gin and the manufacturing of other drinks, as cognac, eggnog and liquors. Until the Dutch East Indonesia got their own government our company sent lots of AVH gin there. Besides that we did export many other brands, but most all of it went to the far east. Also we exported AVH gin, lots of it, to the west coast of America, where the Fremery's (original Dutch people) acted as our salesmen.

"The distillery Hoboken de Bie & Co. is still in Rotterdam. Most everything is now sold in Holland, since Indonesia's freedom. However, we export some of our product to the Phillipines.

A. van Hoboken"

Geraldine Sheehan, Rackerby, sent in the following letter:
HOYT'S GERMAN COLOGNE – E. W. Hoyt & Co., Lowell, Mass. – Copy of letter received from the Lowell City Library, Lowell, Mass. (Dated July 19, 1960)

"This firm was established in January, 1872. E. W. Hoyt & Co. put on the market nearly two million bottles a year. It is no longer in existence."

Mrs. Sheehan also cleared me of possible "lewd" writing in the Medicine Bottle listing:
Forni Magenstarck = Stomach Tonic
Forny's Alpenkrauter Blutbeleber = Mountain Herb Blood Enlivener

Und so, gut friends, mit a vee bit of corn – (with apologies to "Please, Mr. Custer")

> *Thanks Mr. Forni*
> *For your Magenstarck*
> *Since I started taking –*
> *My burps are just a lark.*
>
> or
>
> *His Alpenkrauter Blutbeleber*
> *Changed blood to fast from slow*
> *My wife took some and now believe 'er*
> *She says I gotta go!*

– J.C.T.

## X
## Miscellaneous Information

The November meeting of the ABCAC was held at the Sacramento Garden and Arts Center on Tuesday, November 1, 1960.

Two cases are to be available for bottle displays at the Mineral Society Show November 5th and 6th in the Merchandise Mart at the State Fairgrounds. Don Reich will show his beautiful flasks and whatever else is needed for one case; the Neils, Reibers and Lewises volunteered to fill the other. Mr. Lester spoke about the Mineral Show and said this year's show will be the largest they have ever had, with some 75 exhibits from all over the state, including beautiful crystal and jade.

Mr. and Mrs. Tibbitts spent one Saturday at Sutter's Fort pawing through sacks of broken bits from the excavations that have been going on for a year or so, trying to help identify or date some of the things found. Mr. Tibbitts says they have discovered nearly everything in the Fort is where it shouldn't be. He described some of the fragments to see if anyone could help identify them.

Regarding our own Bottle Show in February — Mrs. Tibbitts, the Scroggins, Keskeys, and Don are the committee. They will hold a meeting next week at the Scroggins' to start their planning. There will be other historical groups showing buttons, dolls, etc.; the whole Garden and Arts building will be utilized. This would be a good opportunity for some of our Associate Members to show some of their collections or at least come to town and meet us and see our bottles.          F. G.

## THIS AND THAT — J.C.T.

The following bit quoted direct from a letter from May Jones, Bishop:

"Papa Eberhard Anheuser started his brew — 1852, so he asked his kinda smart son-in-law to take over — the then Bavarian Breweries — Well, that 'Kid' was smart and things began to pop (corks). So the name Anheuser Busch got applied and finally ended up Anheuser-Busch Brewing Association — eventually cut to Anheuser Busch Brewery in 1879 — Anyhoo — ABCo celebrated its 100th year in 1952 — So there too. The ABGM & Co. came from Bellmont, Nev. I *think* it's the oldest — the man who gave me the dope — suspects AB — but they made all three bottles — (I got the reasons) — The ABGM & Co. neck at least is in the book — it was stoppered then foil over the top — to make it look like champagne. I'm still checking with this gang of bottles — O yeh, they were *not* ever clear — always blue — then they started to the amber — (I have eleven in my set of AB so far). Maybe they sell Anheuser-Busch there—check with the distributors — maybe you'll get the history put out in 1952 on their Beers — It's really a dandy — "Making Friends is Our Business" is the title — I just sent the man who I am writing to, six for their Museum. I'm still missing some — gotta scrounge too — O yeh, I notice by checking my numerous *bottoms* — that AB Co made the bottle for Wright & Taylor Distillers — Louisville, Ky. (All these bottles have the applied necks — I'm talking about — So — If someone finds when the amber bottles were started — that will more than likely help to date the original blue ones — like yours)."

Thanks to Blackie, I have two more old Almanacs in my collection:
DOAN'S DIARY ALMANAC, *1904, Foster-Milburn Co., Publishers, Buffalo, N.Y.;*

DODD'S 1911 ALMANAC, *Buffalo, N.Y.*

The Dodd's 1911 can't help us any because it only advertises Dodd's Kidney Pills, Dodd's Dyspepsia Tablets and Diamond Dinner Pills, and they all came in boxes not bottles. Guess they never heard ABCAC was coming. Anyway – "Diamond Dinner Pills build Muscles, Tone the System, nourish it, Enrich the blood with red corpuscles, Make "Tired Toilers" strong and fit." – *Holy Smokes* –

Doan's 1904 helps us some but never does say how many years prior the products started. It advertises:

| | |
|---|---|
| Doan's Kidney Pills | 50 cents a box |
| Doan's Ointment | 50 cents a box |
| Dr. Thomas' Eclectric Oil | 25 and 50 cents a bottle |
| Dr. Wood's Norway Pine Syrup | 25 and 50 cents a bottle |
| Dr. Fowler's Extract of Wild Strawberry | 25 cents a bottle |
| Burdock Blood Bitters | $1.00 |

Foster-Milburn Co., Proprietors, Buffalo, N.Y.

The Eclectric Oil had been used "for the last fourteen years," so you can get back to 1890 on this.

Frances, if you left the "c" out of "Eclectric," go back and put it in. Evidently this is a misspelling of the word "eclectic" which had an obsolete meaning synonymous with "botanic" in medicine.

Quoting from Doan's 1904: "Mrs. ―― ―― of ―― Thirteenth Street, Sacramento, California, says: "For about two years I never knew the moment when an attack of dull aching and weakness would seat itself just over the loins. I used medicine for it, but it did not agree with my stomach and I stopped the treatment. I was reading one night a Sacramento paper and came across an ad about Doan's Kidney Pills. I said to my husband, to go Ing & Allee's drug store to-morrow and bring me home a box. Half of it relieved me and a continuation of the treatment for a short time longer stopped the last attack. Doan's Kidney Pills are the best medicine I ever used."

Of course this was before Margaret Sanger.

Associate Member Bea Boynton and friend drove all the way down from Quincy and back just to attend our meeting. You were in the pencil draft of the notes but we lost you in typing the master.

Mineral Show was exceptionally good and our two cases of bottles rated right along with the best. *J.C.T.*

# XI
## At Last a Name – "The Pontil"
## and
## 101 Patent Medicines

### THE PONTIL

The December meeting of the Antique Bottle Collector's Association was held at the Sacramento Garden and Arts Center on Tuesday, December 6, 1960.

Mr. Tibbitts started the meeting off by telling us of the first meeting of the Planning Committee for our Bottle Show to be held in February. He asked Jackie Scroggin, Chairman, to give a report regarding this meeting and plans to date.

The question was asked whether or not we would be competing. There will be no competition — the exhibits will be along the line of a flower show, with each family responsible for their own exhibit. Kathryn Ball is going to make some large signs to show various sections, such as "Bitters," "Pop Bottles," "Medicine Bottles," etc. There will also be an "Unclassified" section, and a "Reproduction" section. Then each person will be asked to write a brief description or resume regarding his exhibits. This should make it more interesting to people who are not collectors. If you have beautiful or valuable relics you would like to show, there will be enclosed cases for these.

Bart Huson, Program Chairman, was unable to be at the meeting, but he had Tom Brown show and describe his collection of earthenware or ceramics; Mr. Martin brought quite a collection of bottles found along the railroad track near Truckee; and "Elmer" Lester showed and commented on some things he has found, mainly from the Redevelopment area. "Elmer" also came up with several good suggestions. He says he objects to being called "Mr." Lester, and thinks we should have a hostess at the door to give each person a badge to wear, so that we will learn to know each other's names and become better acquainted. He would also like to suggest that we have a question box in which to drop any questions we would like answered; at each meeting two people could be selected to draw out a question and attempt to answer it at the next meeting. We would in time acquire a lot of information.

He described a trip to Tolinos and said he would be happy to lead a field trip there, where there was an old bottling works. The admission fee to the area of $1.00 entitles you to 5 lbs. of a mineral, the name of which I have forgotten, plus any bottles you may find. Elmer himself came out with about 40.  F.G.

## NOTES FROM J.C.T.

Among some old advertising material I just received is a 5"x 8" picture of Niagara Falls. This is a moonlight scene and in the ever-present vapor at the Horseshoe Falls are the letters spelling out *"Tippecanoe"* (Plate # 8 ). On one of the huge boulders at the foot of the American Falls is written, "Warner's Safe Cure." There must be a good story here here but I don't get it. Care to try?

Another similar size picture shows "Battle of Tippecanoe, 1811." This says, "After once using our 'Tippecanoe' you will use no nostrums nor preparations called 'Bitters,' try 'Tippecanoe' instead." On the back of this picture it shows and I quote "This Cut is a TWO-THIRDS facsimile view of the New Wrapper, which we shall adopt on Oct. 1, 1883, to protect our patrons from the fraudulent imitations with which the market is flooded. Hereafter we shall put up a Kidney, Liver, Urinary, etc., Preparation, in this Wrapper, under the name of "Warner's 'SAFE' Cure" (see pages 31 and 32), but we shall also continue to put up our medicine for old patrons, in "Warner's 'SAFE' Kidney and Liver Cure" wrappers. The Title "Warner's 'SAFE' Cure" is preferred to "Warner's 'SAFE' Kidney and Liver Cure," because it is not so confusing to customers who wish easily to distinguish the real "SAFE Remedies" from the imitations."

Please notice that these notes now have a name — "The Pontil." Mrs. T. thought this up and even I think it is good. The pontil was used

 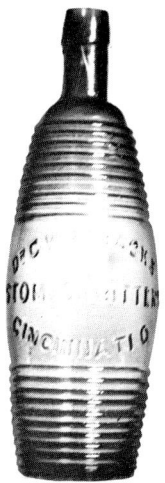 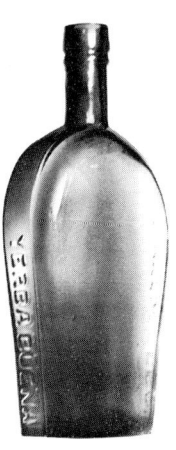 

PLATE 3. Left to right. BITTERS.

- 9½" high, barrel, amber, BIMAL.
  F – OLD SACHEM BITTERS AND WIGWAM TONIC

- 9¼" high, barrel, amber, BIMAL.
  F – DR. C.W. ROBACK'S STOMACH BITTERS
  CINCINNATI. O

- 8¼" high, flask, amber, BIMAL.
  L – YERBA BUENA
  R – BITTERS, S.F. CAL.

- 8-7/8" high, square, amber green, BIMAL.
  F – DR. J. HOSTETTER'S STOMACH BITTERS

PLATE 4. Left to right. PATENT MEDICINES.

- 4" high, round, aqua, BIMALOP.
  F – ANDERSON'S DERMADOR

- 9" high, rect., aqua, BIMAL.
  F – HOOD'S SARSAPARILLA
  B – APOTHOCARIES
  L – C.I. HOOD & CO.
  R – LOWELL, MASS.

- 8" high, rect., aqua, BIMAL.
  F – THE GREAT DR. KILMER'S SWAMP ROOT KIDNEY LIVER & BLADDER CURE SPECIFIC
  R – DR. KILMER & CO.
  L – BINGHAMPTON, N.Y.

- 8½" high, oval, aqua, BIMAL.
  F – LYDIA E. PINKHAM'S VEGETABLE COMPOUND

- 10½" high, square taper, honey amber, BIMAL.
  F – EXPECTORAL   (vertical)
       WILD CHERRY TONIC   (45 degree and upside down)
  L – ROHRER'S
  R – LANCASTER P[a]

by the glass blower to hold the article up while part of the work was done. "The Pontil" will be used by your "gas blower" (editor) to help hold the club up.

That's all the Tidbits for this time, but I am enclosing a list of 100 Patent Medicines I hope you find interesting.

A Happy New Year to Each and Every One of You — but don't get carried away. I want to see each one of you on Tuesday, January 3, 1961, at our meeting. Let's start this year out with a bang and our empty bottles, not with a bust emptying bottles. *J.C.T.*

## ONE HUNDRED STANDARD PATENT MEDICINES

ABBEY'S EFFERVESCENT SALT
    For sluggish liver and attendant disorders.

ARLINGTON CHEMICAL CO.'s PEPTONOIDS
    In liquid and powder forms. A food in convenient forms for weak digestion.

AUBERGIER'S LACTUCARIUM SYRUP AND LOZENGES
    For coughs, colds, hoarseness, and so forth.

ANTIPHLOGISTINE
    A clay in ointment form for absorbing inflammation.

AYER'S CATHARTIC PILLS
    Laxative, cathartic, and so forth.

AYER'S CHERRY PECTORAL
    For various affections of the lungs and throat.

AYER'S SARSAPARILLA
    For complaints arising from impurities of the blood.

BEECHAM'S PATENT PILLS
    For torpid liver, indigestion, and so forth.

BLAIR'S RHEUMATIC AND GOUT PILLS
    For rheumatism, gout, and so forth.

BRANDRETH'S PILLS
    Laxative, cathartic, sour stomach, and so forth.

BROWN'S BRONCHIAL TROCHES
    For coughs, colds, hoarseness and bronchial irritation.

BULL'S COUGH SYRUP
    For coughs, colds, and so forth.

CARTER'S LITTLE LIVER PILLS
    For biliousness, torpid liver, constipation, sallow skin, and so forth.

CASCARETS
    A candy cathartic for chronic constipation.

CASTORIA
    For assimilating the food and regulating the stomach and bowels of infants and children.

CROSBY'S VITALIZED PHOSPHITES
    Brain and nerve food. Useful in the deficient mental and bodily growth of infants and children.

CUTICURA RESOLVENT
    For purifying the blood.

CUTICURA
    A salve for eruptions of the skin and unrivaled as a hair dressing.

DELAVAU'S WHOOPING COUGH REMEDY
    For whooping cough and croup.

DENTACURA
    An antiseptic and detergent tooth paste.

ELY'S CREAM BALM
    For catarrh, catarrhal deafness, hay fever and cold in the head.
EMERSON'S BROMO-SELTZER
    For nervous headache, sleeplessness, over-fatigue, and so forth.
ENTONA (HEALTH FOOD CO.'S WHITE WHEAT GLUTEN SUPPOSI-
TORIES — For hemorrhoids and constipation.
FAIRCHILD'S PANOPEPTON
    A food composed of beef and wheat in soluble and absorbable form.
FELLOW'S COMPOUND SYRUP OF HYPOPHOSPHITES
    An ideal reconstructive tonic.
GLYCO-THYMOLINE (KRESS)
    An alkaline antiseptic and non-irritating solution.
GRAY'S GLYCERINE TONIC COMPOUND
    For diseases of chest and throat. Useful where stomack is weak.
GREEN'S AUGUST FLOWER
    For dyspepsia in all forms.
GUDE'S PEPTO-MANGAN
    A widely-known and prescribed tonic.
H.H.H. MEDICINE
    A liniment for general purposes for man or beast.
HAGEE'S COD-LIVER OIL CORDIAL
    A tonic stimulant in palatable form.
HANCE BROS. AND WHITE'S PHENOL-SODIQUE
    An antiseptic and disinfectant for all purposes.
HAINE'S GOLDEN SPECIFIC
    Recommended for intemperance.
HEISKELL'S OINTMENT
    For tetter, erysipelas and eruptions of the skin.
HEMBALOIDS
    A blood enricher and alterative.
HEMPEPTONE
    Organic iron. A useful tonic.
HOFF'S EXTRACT OF MALT
    A stimulant and aid to weak digestion.
HOLMES' FRAGRANT FROSTILLA
    A useful toilet article.
HOOD'S SARSAPARILLA
    An alterative, tonic and blood purifier.
HUMPHREY'S MARVEL OF HEALING
    A pure distillate of witch-hazel recommended for household and stable uses.
HUMPHREY'S WITCH HAZEL OIL
    A hemorrhoidal and general salve.
JAYNE'S ALTERATIVE
    As it is called a good alterative.
JAYNE'S CARMINATIVE BALSAM
    For dysentery, diarrhea, cholera morbus, sick headache, etc.
JAYNE'S EXPECTORANT
    For coughs, colds, bronchial affections and irritations.
JAYNE'S SANATIVE PILLS
    For constipation and disorders of the liver.
JAYNE'S TONIC VERMIFUGE
    For removal of worms and an aid to digestion.
JOHNSON'S DIGESTIVE TABLETS

For dyspepsia and indigestion.
JUNIPER TAR (WHITEHURST'S)
   For colds, distressing cough, irritations of bronchial tubes and mucous membranes.
KEASBEY AND MATTISON CO.'S ALKALITHIA
   A handy effervescent salt for all forms of rheumatism.
KEASBEY AND MATTISON CO.'S BROMO-CAFFEINE
   A handy effervescent salt for brain workers.
KILMER'S SWAMP ROOT
   For acute and chronic kidney and liver disease.
MALTINE
   A concentrated extract of malted barley, wheat and oats. An efficient aid to sound and healthy digestion.
LACTOPEPTINE
   An aid to perfect digestion. In powder, liquid or tablet form.
LAVILLE'S GOUT REMEDY
   For rheumatic and gouty disorders.
LAXATIVE BROMO-QUININE TABLETS
   A remedy for coughs, colds and headache.
LISTERINE
   A widely used antiseptic, prophylactic and disinfectant.
NATURAL CARLSBAD SALT
   An effervescent salt known as nature's aperient.
OMEGA OIL
   A household liniment for aches, pains and soreness.
OSGOOD'S INDIA CHOLAGOGUE
   For malaria, chills and fever, and so forth.
PAINE'S CELERY COMPOUND
   A nerve tonic, active alterative, laxative and diuretic.
PERUNA
   A tonic used in catarrhal, dyspeptic and kidney disorders.
PHILLIP'S EMULSION OF COD-LIVER OIL
   Phillip's emulsion of cod-liver oil. A valuable remedy combined with wheat phosphates.
PHILLIP'S MILK OF MAGNESIA
   A mild laxative and an excellent dentifrice.
PHOSPHAGON
   A natural nerve nutrient.
PIERCE'S FAVORITE PRESCRIPTION
   For chronic weaknesses of women.
PIERCE'S GOLDEN MEDICAL DISCOVERY
   A remedy for chronic or lasting ailments.
PINKHAM'S VEGETABLE COMPOUND
   A remedy for diseases of women.
POND'S EXTRACT
   A reliable remedy for many purposes.
RADWAY'S READY RELIEF
   Used externally as a liniment and internally as a counter-irritant.
RESINAL
   An ointment for all forms of inflammations, eruptions and irritations of the skin.
RIPANS TABULES
   For stomach disorders.
RULLSELL EMULSION

A tonic composed of mixed fats or oils.
SAGE'S CATARRH REMEDY
For catarrh, hay fever, influenza, and so forth.
SANITOL
A liquid, paste or powder for the teeth.
SANTAL-MIDY CAPSULES
For venereal diseases.
SCHENCK'S MANDRAKE PILLS
For biliousness and liver complaint.
SCHENCK'S PULMONIC SYRUP
For consumption, diseases of the lungs and respiratory organs.
SCHENCK'S SEAWEED TONIC
For dyspepsia.
SCOTT'S EMULSION OF COD-LIVER OIL
For pulmonary diseases, coughs, colds and general debility.
SHEFFIELD'S CREAM DENTIFRICE
A paste for cleansing the teeth.
SLOAN'S LINIMENT
Known as the "Killer of Pain."
SLOCUM'S COLT'S FOOT EXPECTORANT
For coughs, colds, influenza, and so forth.
SLOCUM'S OZOMULSION
For throat, chest and lung troubles, a flesh and strength producer.
SLOCUM'S PSYCHINE
For disorders of throat and lungs.
SOZODONT
For preserving, cleansing the teeth and hardening the gums.
STEARN'S WINE OF COD-LIVER OIL
A palatable compound of cod-liver oil and iron.
STUART'S SYDPEPSIA TABLETS
For stomach and intestinal indigestion or dyspepsia.
SWAIM'S PANACEA
A very old and widely known blood purifier.
SWAYNE'S OINTMENT
For tetter, itch, ringworm and eruptions of the skin.
SWAYNE'S PANACEA
For all forms of blood humors.
SWIFT'S SPECIFIC
A blood purifier for syphilitic disorders.
SYRUP OF FIGS
For habitual constipation.
TARRANT'S SELTZER APERIENT
For indigestion, headache and constipation.
THYMOZONE
An antiseptic and prophylactic for internal and external uses.
VAPO-CRESOLENE
A remedy for whooping cough, asthma, catarrh, and so forth.
VIN MARIANA
A coca wine tonic.
WAMPOLE'S PREPARATION OF COD-LIVER OIL
In a tasteless form; tonic for all wasting diseases.
WARNER'S BROMO SODA
For headache, sleeplessness, and so forth.

WARNER'S SAFE CURE
   For kidney and liver diseases.
WAMPOLE'S ANTISEPTIC SOLUTION
   A valuable antiseptic and germicide.
WALTHER'S PEPTONIZED PORT
   For all forms of dyspepsia, malnutrition, and so forth.
WILLIAMS' PINK PILLS
   A blood builder and nerve tonic.
WYETH'S BEEF, IRON AND WINE
   A nutritive tonic for impaired nutrition, impoverished blood and general debility.

The above listing was taken from a book (and what a book) given me by a co-worker, Russell Anderson. To help you date the above bottles, this book was published in 1901.

## XII
## The Bottle Bug
## by
## Lavine Layton

THE PONTIL

January 3, 1961 — first meeting in 1961 of the Antique Bottle Collector's Association, at Sacramento Garden and Arts Center, and surprisingly well attended for so early in the year.

Mr. Tibbitts reports that the Cope brothers, though very busy in their new "Firehouse," still wish to belong to the ABCA. This "Firehouse" is a pretty fabulous place according to those who have visited it. Heard they had to get special permission from the ABC to use their beautiful crystal decanters behind the bar.

Elmer Lester wants to arrange a field trip to Tolenos. It would be nice to wait for some sunny weather (what's that?) but it was thought we could meet at Vacaville and go on from there together (only 4 miles). There are 4 mining claims there where they mine travertine, which is used to make ceramic tile. The $1.00 admission entitles each visitor to take out 10 pounds of this material (and any empty bottles you may find are free). This was the site of an old resort, "Tolenos Springs." There are no buildings any more, but Elmer brought out 40 bottles on one trip. January 22 was set as a tentative date — check with Elmer on the 21st to find out if we are going — then meet at the Milk Farm at 10 a.m.; we'll leave together from there not later than 10:30.

Very few forms have been turned in indicating participation in the bottle show February 4th and 5th. We are all going to have to get behind this "Journey Into the Past," to make it a success. Jackie Scroggin, Chairman, set up a sample "unclassified" exhibit to stimulate ideas.
F.G.

THIS AND THAT — J.C.T.

Margie Thompson arranged for the hostesses for the show. Thanks, Margie.

Your duties are: 1. Be there, 2. Tell the nice kids hands off, 3. Wear your host or hostess bottle badge being made by Katherine Ball, 4. Tell the kids to put their hands in their pockets, 5. Pass out to interested people slips that I will prepare telling about our club and how to join, 6. Watch those darn kids, 7. Answer questions if you can, 8. Remember, those bottles you save may be your own.

Jackie Scroggin has been doing a wonderful job getting publicity on the show, in the Bee, the Union, the Shopper, antique store windows, library exhibit, TV show, etc. Credit here also due Lillian Jorgenson, Elmer Lester, Grace Neil, Darlene Piggott. Thanks, all.

Mrs. T. has been on the phone discussing exhibits with you members. Thanks. What I want and feel we should have is a show that is representative of the bottles of all club members; *not just the best or the oldest*. This variety will be of more interest to a greater number of people. What isn't appreciated by the few who may know an old bottle will be enjoyed by even more people on a reminiscent basis — "My mother used that when I was a boy."

Hello, you out-of-towners. We are looking forward to seeing all of you at this show. Using you for an excuse we are planning an evening get-together (to be sure we find one another) on Saturday night, February 4th. This will be from 9:30 p.m. on, in a very historic spot in Sacramento — the old original Firehouse #3, 1112 TWO Street. (This is not the best end of town, but interesting, so — "K" Street is One Way west; go west on "K" past 2nd Street and turn left into alley between 2nd and Front; there you will find a big, lighted parking lot and a rear entrance.) Tell them, "Joe sent me." Here you will find a bar recreated in an atmosphere of the best of the old west. It makes me expect to hear Pallidin call "Hey Boy" any minute. This is a "no host" affair, or in plain English, check your guns at the door and pay your own way!

Here is some information from Faith Graham, Colusa:

"Hansen and Kahler were in business from 1896 to 1907. They were a bottling company, not a brewery. They bottled Budweiser beer for Anheiser-Busch. The light bottles that had AB in them were discontinued after prohibition. The beer would spoil if set in the sun, so they then used the brown bottles for their beer. They — H.K. — sold out to the Buffalo brewery of Sacramento. They also bottled beer for Buffalo. They had their plant in Oakland, California.

"The bottles were marked with Hansen and Kahler, and this was done by a stone. A man marked the bottles by hand using equipment that was like dental equipment."

Now to summarize some of the information sent in for the club card files by Researcher Geraldine Sheehan, Rackerby.

In 1872 *Fred Raschen* went with Weinreich, Lohse & Co., 514 J St., Sacramento, wholesale liquor dealers. After changing to Weinreich & Bartels and then to H. Weinreich & Co., Mr. Raschen became a partner and later on purchased the business at which time the name changed to Fred Raschen Wholesale Liquors. In 1907 the business was incorporated under the name of F.Raschen & Company. This firm went out of business in 1918.

*Roth and Company* were importers of wholesale wines and liquors, 214 Pine St., San Francisco. Began as Roth & Videane in 1868, changed to Roth & Levy in '76, to Roth and Company in '79. 1888 was last appearance of name in San Francisco City Directory.

In 1870 H. H. Warner & Co. started their remedy business. After Warner sold his interest in it, it became the Warner Safe Cure Co., and later on the Warner Safe Remedies Co. and selling Warner's Safe Cure, W.S. Pills, W.S. Rheumatic Cure, W.S. Diabetes Cure, W.S. Asthma Cure, Warner's Tippecanoe the Best, Warner's Tippecanoe XXX, W.S. Nervine, W.S. Pills.   Thanks, Mrs. Sheehan.

We picked a good day for our Tolenas Springs field trip and those of you who missed it missed a darn good time. Making the trip were the Riebers, Willi Vidak, Elmer Lester, the Jorgensons, the Neils, Mrs. Croxen and the Demings, Frances Gwynne, the Zooks, the Thompsons and the Tibbitts. Perfect bottling conditions prevailed and the following finds recorded – *Sodas:* Tolenas, Jackson's, Phillip's, Priest's, Walter's, Golden's G.A., Oakland Steam, Samuel's, Solano.  *Misc:* Ehman Olive Oil, Vasoline, Glycerole, Dr. Ward's, G.A. Root's Orange Laxative, and many old "say nothings."

'Twas a good day, good people, good bottling. Thanks, Elmer. – *J.C.T.*

### "The Bottle Bug"
#### by Lavine Layton

*All day I tramp the burning sands,*
*Crawl through brush and barbed wire strands,*
*Rip my jeans and scratch my hands.*
*The misery I go through.*
  *I seek and search and prowl and pry.*
*I shake and freeze or sweat and fry.*
*I dig and delve, down low, up high.*
*There's NOTHING I don't do.*
  *Abandoned mines, deserted homes,*
*Where varmints prowl and lone winds moan,*
*Through old, old dumps and quarry stones*
*That bruise me black and blue*
  *I trespass, where the signs say "No!"*
*I cannot stop, but on must go,*
*To yonder spot, where old boards show.*
*A homestead this place knew.*
  *With lusty vigor, I apply*
*My trusty digger, and as I*
*Make trash and rusty tin cans fly,*
*My hopes flare up anew,*
  *For here are chips of colored glass,*
*Broken bits of purple-ness,*
*And now my heart starts beating fast,*
*At last. Can it be true?*
  *Oh! Fate, be kind to me, I pray.*
*I've come a long and weary way*
*To this lone spot, at end of day.*
*And now, I beg of you,*
  *Let it be perfect! Round or square!*
*Let every little bit be there,*
*No cracks, nor chips, not anywhere!*
*That's all I ask of you!*
  *The sun has sunk behind the trees,*
*It's nearly most too dark to see,*
*As I sink down, on trembling knees,*

> To get a better view!
> And there, at last, my treasure lies!
> I gaze with fond, adoring eyes.
> With loving hands, I claim my prize,
> My long, long search is through!
> What is my treasure, do you ask?
> And now that it is mine, at last,
> Was it worthwhile, the awful task?
> Well, I will answer you!
> Its worth, is just to me alone.
> To have, to hold, to carry home.
> To show with pride, my very own.
> As no one else can do.
> To scrub, to rub, to clean with care.
> With sand and bottle brush, so there
> Will be no speck, nor stain, nowhere,
> To mar its sun-turned hue.
> No chest of gold, nor precious stones,
> No flower rare, nor fossil bones.
> Just glass, on which the sun has shone.
> How long? I wish I knew.
> A purple bottle! Yes, that's it!
> And now I find that I can't quit.
> But must hunt on, for I've been bit,
> By the Bottle Bug, like you.

# XIII
# Complete Listing of Soda
# (Pop) Bottle Inventory

The March meeting of ABCAC was held at the Sacramento Garden and Arts Center on Tuesday, March 7, 1961.

Our program chairman, Bart Huson, gave a fine talk on the soda works bottles.

Lillian Jorgensen had a good summary on the Buffalo Brewing Company.

Mrs. Huson made some cards pertaining to some bottles and the owners of the company who made them.

Mrs. Mix had a lot to tell about the Mason Jars. We thank her for the wonderful talk and the good information.

Dr. George Yeager had some good pieces of purple glass. He told us the purpling of glass is dependent on manganese.

Am including in these notes, a summary of what Marie and Lillian presented. Not enough room to cover everything now. Will try to cover the others in later notes.

Those of you who didn't get to town to the show missed a real good thing. Attendance-wise it was the biggest show ever put on in the Garden and Arts Center. Over 4,300 checked through during the two days. 1,000 has been considered a good two-day show. Although our bottles were the main part of the show, the buttons, dolls, arrangements and historical exhibits played no small part in making it a very interesting and beautiful show.

My thanks to all of you who exhibited and/or otherwise helped in making this show such a success.

There were 45 of us that got together at the Firehouse Saturday night; many local members and some from Carson City, Quincy, Rackerby, Galt, Herald and Bangor. A few of us didn't have any more sense than to go from there to Shaky's for beer, pizza and "Dixieland" music. Oh well, someone has to provide bottles for the future Bottlers of America.

Mrs. T. dug up a perfect *"Pretzel Bottle"* (Plate #16) a couple of Sundays ago. It is just like the one pictured in Maust. This Sacramento dump was evidently used from about 1890 and we know it was closed in 1920.

More books for Elmer to add to our book reference card file and for you people to find and enjoy. The ABC's of Old Glass, Carl W. Dreppherd, Doubleday & Co., 1949; Early American Bottles and Flasks, Stephen Van Renselaer, Transcript Printing Co., 1926; Those Were the Good Old Days, Edgar R. Jones, Simon & Schuster, 1959.

Our new members, the Kreiss's of Woodside, have these books among others. The first covers just what it says; the second is the hard-to-obtain, out-of-print book by Van Renselaer that is referred to by McKearin and others. The third is a large collection of old interesting advertising.

There must be honor among bottlers as well as thieves because these new members loaned this Van Renselaer book to the Georgi's and ourselves. We have had it first and if these notes don't get out, it is the Kreiss's fault. We think we have identified that little pontil marked flask that Lee Scroggins dug in the west end as a snuff bottle.

There have been some wonderful finds in Sacramento's west end lately, namely on TWO Street in case you haven't heard. Many pontil scarred bottles, many old pops with graphite smoothed bases, etc., etc. Some of the lucky members were Lee Scroggins, Fred Piggott, Frank Thornburg, Ed Hughes, Mike and Joe Kelly, and Rick Wallace. This is a real mining operation and a six-foot-deep hole is the usual thing. Good luck, folks, that's about three feet too deep for me.

Here is some information gotten together for us by Marie Huson and taken from various year issues of "Industries of San Francisco."

The Humboldt Brewery, S.F. "The manufacture last year was over 8,000 barrels and will be greatly increased in 1884."

F. Chevalier and Co. A wholesale liquor house in San Francisco, founded in 1860. Sole agents for E. Mercier & Co. Champagnes, and sole proprietor of Castle Distillery, Kentucky.

Wichman and Lutgen, S.F., founded in 1876, handled wines, brandies, whiskies, mineral waters, cordials, ales, etc.; also manufacturers of Dr. Foster's Alpine Stomach Bitters; also represent these whiskies: Old Gilt Edge, Joseph Hooper's Identical Old Bourbon 1859, Hood and Hyden's H & H Rye Whiskey.

Walters Bros. & Co., S.F., founded in 1866, importers of brandies, wines and gins; sole proprietors of Oregon Grape Root Bitters; specialized in Horseshoe and C.B. Cook Kentucky Whiskies.

Wm. T. Coleman & Co., founded in Placerville in 1849 and in 1850 moved to S.F. Sole agents for Old Horsey Rye, Daniel Lawrence & Sons' Rum, Wolfe's Aromatic Schnapps, and Kennedy's East India Bitters.

Hencken & Schrodder, S.F., Distributors of Old Kentucky Bourbon,

O.K., and Our Choice; also sole agent for Dr. Schrader's Famous Hamburg Bitters. (1884 book)

John Keeny, S.F., Distributors of Sheridan Bourbon. (1884 book)

Denaveaux and Maison, S.F., Agency for Jockey Club Bourbon, Old Crown Bourbon, and Royal Bourbon. (Over 30 years old in 1884)

Boca Brewing Co., S.F., started in 1875 with a brewery in Boca, Calif. Sold throughout the Pacific Coast, Mexico, Central and South America, Hawaiian Islands, Japan and China.

"Boca Por La Boca," the Mexicans would say, "Cause who would want Tequilla, on such a hot dry day?" Sorry, don't blame Marie for this, blame me, J.C.T.

Alfred Grennbaum & Co., S.F., Importers of: Crescent Bourbon, Keystone Monogram Rye, Bourgeaux Wines, Rhine Wines, Wilhelms Quele Blue Label Mineral Water, Hardy Cognac, Cantrell & Cochrane Ginger Ale, Hazards Cider and Hazards Handsome Man. (1887 book)

Marie, thank you from all of us for this research information.

Now for the material presented at the meeting by Lillian Jorgenson on the Buffalo Brewery. Herman F. Graw, born in Germany, 1846; to U.S., 1863; 1871, married brewer's daughter in Buffalo, N.Y. and became a member of firm, Liegle's. Sold out in 1887 and came to California. Selected Sacramento as site for brewery which he wanted to be the largest and the best in the country. Head Brewer was Baptiste Nierendorf who had a diploma from the celebrated Brewer's Academy in Germany. Brewery started in 1889, capacity 60,000 BBLs, cost $400,000.00, closed 1929.

Also from L.J. The El Dorado Brewery in Stockton started in 1853 and closed in 1955.

Also, Martini was the name given to a drink by a bartender in Martinez.

"The termite came up to the bar and asked the barmaid, 'Is the bar tender here?'" ... J.C.T.

If any of you have that rather modern but beautiful ruby red bottle made by Anchor-Hocking, hang on to it. Bea Boynton wrote to the company to see if she could get more of these and I quote part of the reply she received. "We are, however, very sorry to inform you that we discontinued manufacturing Ruby Red glass bottles many years ago and unfortunately, we do not have even one sample bottle of that color."

New member Quigley of Quincy sent in some good information which I will give to George R. for our blue research cards; I will summarize here. All taken from 1870 and 1871 Saturday Evening Posts. Some of this by Alice Fountain also.

Rimmels Perfumery. Oriental aspersor for sprinkling perfumes.

Lea & Perrins showing the old neck and stopper.

White Glycerine for bleaching the skin. Horseshoe trademark.

Walker's Vinegar Bitters. "Immediate and certain help for all the sick."

Brown's Vermifuge Comfits. Burnett's Kalliston. Burnett's Cologne Water. Rimmels Toilet Vinegar (also good for mosquito bites). Polands White Pine Compound. Burnett's Flavoring Extracts. Burnett's Cocoaine (best and cheapest hairdressing in the world). Waynes Diuretic & Alterative. Choraline (for calm sleep). White's Specialty for Dyspepsia.

Vegetable Pulmonary Balsama (1826 to 1870). Whitcomb's Asthma

Remedy Sure Cure. Humbold's Extract Buchu. Pratt's Astral Oil. Franham's Asthma Cure. Dr. Kennedy's Hair Tea. Congress and Empire Spring Waters. Atwood's Quinine Tonic Bitters.

From 1901 Sports Afield: Three-In-One "The only gun oil." From 1911 Life: Eureka Stomach Bitters. White Rock (World's Best Table Water). Old Overholt Rye. Martell's Brandy. Caroni Bitters. Red Raven. Pabst Extract.

Thanks, Lorraine and Alice. Info such as this sure does help us date and identify our bottles.

Received a nice letter from Lavine Layton, Redding, giving me permission to use her Bottle Bug poem in my book. (Am in Chapter 10, six more to go, any orders?) She is writing another poem and will send it in when finished. This I am looking forward to.

George Rieber has given me a listing of the pop bottles that were turned in on the last inventory.

```
B .......................................... 1
B & H........................................ 1
Bay City Soda Water Company, S.F................. 1
The Belfast Ginger Ale Company, S.F.............. 1
E. L. Billings, Sac City........................ 5
Bluelick Water ................................ 1
J. Boardwan – Mineral Water..................... 1
Bremenkampf & Regli – Eureka, Nevada ............. 3
C & R Eagle Soda Works – Sac City ................ 1
Phil Caduc Napa Soda........................... 2
California Bottling Works, 407 K Street, Sacramento....... 2
Cantrell & Cochrane, Dublin & Belfast (round bottom) ..... 2
Casey & Cronnan, Eagle Soda Works................ 2
Hugh Casey, Eagle Soda Works ................... 3
Owen Casey, Eagle Soda Works, Sac City............. 4
M. Cronan – Sacramento, California ............... 1
Crystal Distilled Pure Water Company, Berkeley, California.. 1
Eagle Bottling Works – Tacoma, Washington ......... 1
Empire Soda Works, San Francisco ................ 1
Eureka, California Soda Water Company, S.F........... 1
J. A. Farrell – Grass Valley..................... 1
Richard J. Floyd – New York .................... 1
Golden Gate................................... 1
Good's Patent ................................. 1
Holden's Crystal Soda Works – Sacramento ........... 1
Holden's GA Capitol Soda Works, Sacramento........... 1
Jackson's Napa Soda Springs .................... 6
Kern Company Bottling Works .................... 1
Levy Brothers – Portland, Oregon ................. 1
Lion Soda Works – Walnut Grove .................. 1
H. Mau & Company – Eureka, Nevada ................ 2
Majestic Bottling Company – San Francisco............ 1
Mokolumne Hills Soda Works ..................... 1
Nevada City Soda Works    E.T.R. Powell ............ 1
Oakland Pioneer Soda Water Company ................ 1
Oakland Steam Soda Works ........................ 1
Oakland Soda Works.............................. 1
```

| | |
|---|---|
| J.C. Parker & Sons, New York | 1 |
| Peerless Ginger Ale Company, S.F. | 1 |
| Pioneer Soda Works — S.F. | 3 |
| Henry J. Postel — Capital Soda Works | 1 |
| Postel & Schneer — Sacramento, California | 1 |
| Priest Napa Valley Soda | 1 |
| Priest Natural Soda | 2 |
| Priest Soda | 1 |
| Ross's Belfast (round bottom) | 2 |
| Samuel Soda Springs | 1 |
| C. Schneer & Company — Sacramento, California | 2 |
| Shasta Ginger Ale | 1 |
| Star Soda Works, Sacramento | 1 |
| P.J. Sullivan — Santa Rosa | 1 |
| Summit Mineral Water | 1 |
| Sunrise Soda Works — Sacramento, California | 1 |
| Tolenas Soda Springs | 6 |
| Toulomne Soda Works | 1 |
| Walter's Napa County Soda | 1 |
| C.A. Werle Mok Hill | 1 |
| Henry J. Winkle — Sacramento, California | 1 |
| Williams Bros. — San Jose, California | 1 |
| Yreka Bottling Works | 1 |
| Zeis & Sons — Redding, California | 1 |
| Vincent Hathaway & Company  Ginger Ale Boston (round bottom) | 1 |

I have a lot more Almanacs and Trade Cards now and am using them for material in my book. Here is some information from Ayer's American Almanac for the use of Farmers, Planters, Mechanics, Mariners, and All Families 1868.

Their first Almanac was put out in 1853 at which time only their Cherry Pectoral was widely known. Of this product the Almanac states, "It is an anodyne expectorant, gently assisting the throat and lungs in throwing off the morbific matter, and at the same time allaying the irritation which causes the abnormal action of those organs."

Sample of humor: "A man, charged with ten gallons of molasses in an eight-gallon keg, said he did not care for the money, only it was such a strain on the keg." "It is said that hoops surround the loveliest of all things, — girls and whiskey."

"The certificates of cures by our Compound Extract of Sarsaparilla, of which we have published volumes in former years, show convincingly that it is a specific antidote in nearly, if not quite, all cases of scrofulous contamination."

Ayer's Cathartic Pills. (This is the little bottle saying Ayer's Pills.) Advertised as being good for many, many ailments.

Ayer's Ague Cure. "For the relief and cure of Ague, Fever and Ague, Chills and Fever, or Intermittent Fever." This disease arises from miasm emitted by moist ground containing vegetable matter in process of decomposition."

Ayer's Hair Vigor. (This is the flat, ugly, odd-shaped bottle that says Ayer's on the bottom.) "It is a delightful dressing, rendering the hair soft, pliant, and glossy, and perfuming it with a new odor of rare delicacy, much admired by all who have used it." Wonder what two dabs would do?

From another Almanac:
Sunny day, Skies are clear. Hip, Hooray! Spring is here.
Flannels off, Dismal day. Cold and cough, Pneumoni-a.
Flannels on, Hot as fire. Sigh and groan, and perspire
Horrid fever! Awful chills! O! My Liver! HERRICK'S PILLS.

## XIV
## 121 Families in the Club at This Point

The meeting was called to order at 8:15, April 4, 1961.
### THIS AND THAT – J.C.T.

Lots of new members. Welcome. Am devoting most of this Pontil space to listing of all members — so, not much other info, sorry. Use this member list this summer and look up your fellow bottlers. Watch out for the horsetraders!

Here's some info from Alice Osborne, Redding:

Zeis & Sons of Redding had their bottling works on Oregon Street in Redding in the 1897's.

Also Cone & Co. had a bottling works in Red Bluff. A friend has a soda water bottle from there, and also one marked R.B. and Cone Co. This was also in the '70's and '80's.

As for the Hunyadi Janos Bitterquelle that I mentioned before, Johnnie, my husband, copied the name off the bottle, took it to the Central Valley High School where he works and the history teacher looked it up, and came up with the information about Gen. Janos Hunyadi of the late 13th Century.

In 1863, H. A. Wiser established the Buckeye Wine Cellar and Distillery. Buckeye is a small mining town north and west of Redding.

Quote from letter from W. J. Mathews, General Manager of Brock Glass Co., Ltd.

"Potash glass is more likely to contain manganese and therefore more likely to 'purple.' Soda-lime glass is used for bottles and cheaper glassware. Sunlight will turn it to a straw color, and sometimes almost an amber, depending on the amount of selenium used.

"Pot glass was common up to 1915. Such glass, therefore, is more likely to contain manganese. Glass with lead in its composition, must be decolorized with manganese, and will turn purple in the sun. Lead and selenium combine to turn glass brown."

Thanks a lot, Alice.

Mrs. T. visited two glass factories in Mexico, one in Mexico City and one in Tlaquepaque (Tlakipaki). At the latter one, Fabrica De Vidrio Tipico (Typical Glass Factory) she bought me a Tortuga Verde (green turtle) for 20 pesos ($1.60) and a Batador (muddler) for 2 pesos (16¢).

At the Fabrica De Vidrio in M.C. she bought me a hand-blown bottle, 15 pesos, a beautiful blue blobular ash tray, 10 pesos, and 6 crazy misshapen and odd colored hand-blown glasses, 15 pesos.

So any of you guys feeling jealous about the $4.96 worth of beautiful Mexican glass I got — just give your wife $500 and send her to Mexico. Pays off about as well as my trips to Nevada for bottles at that!

Have seen and heard of more beautiful old bottles coming out of Sacramento's west end. Took a trip down through there today. Holy smokes!! The Chinese could have gotten to some of those bottles easier. The only way I could compete with Gopher Brown, Mole Scroggins, Badger Wallace, and the like would be to rent a power shovel. *J.C.T.*

## XV
## The Cache of Placer Pete
## by
## Lavine Layton

The meeting was called to order, May 2, 1961.

John read a letter from the Annual Conference of California Historical Societies, inviting our President to speak on Antique Bottles at their Annual Conference to be held in the Fallon Theatre, Columbia State Park, June 22 through 24. This talk will be part of a panel on "Organizations about which We Ought to Know More." They expect from 150 to 200 delegates to attend. John graciously accepted.

Ed Hughes sent a list of his collection of Bitter Bottles (word Bitters in the glass); he has 81 different types.

Marie Huson brought some literature and material for Geo. Reiber, for the files; e.g. Walker's Vinegar Bitters started in Stockton, then moved to New York.

Sturgill carefully extricated a Cannon Bottle from inside his jacket that he had found at the Shaw Ranch near Murphys. It held "Big Gun Gin" (very beautiful and *very* valuable).

Edith Tibbitts told about visiting glass factories in Mexico — we are all very glad to have Edy back.

Meeting adjourned to view a 24-minute movie of the Story Behind the Bottle, procured by our Program Chairman, Mr. Huson.

*Wilhelmina Vidak, Secretary*

### THIS AND THAT — *J.C.T.*

Many thanks to Bart Huson for obtaining the 24-minute 16mm Eastmancolor sound film on bottles for us. This was entitled "The Story Behind A Bottle" and showed the evolution of bottle making from the old, old days right up to the present. It was really worth seeing and made the different types of bottles mean more to us I am sure.

Marie Huson brought us a pamphlet "Sources of Information on Glass — Glassmaking — Glass Containers." This is put out by the Glass Container Manufacturers Institute, Inc., 99 Park Avenue, New York 16, New York. Try sending for it.

Basement excavation at 4th & L has been producing for a few of the members lately. Down there once, saw many nice fragments but the best we came up with was a Tolenas soda Mrs. T. dug up. Loren Zook came up with a small pumpkinseed flask, a Peruna bottle, an old Sac drug store bottle and others. Ran into Larry Cope there and he said he also had gotten a few there.

PLATE 5. Left to right. SODAS.

- 7¼" high, round, cobalt blue, BIMAL.
  F – NAPA SODA
  B – NATURAL MINERAL WATER
- 7" high, round, cobalt blue, BIMAL.
  F – C. & K.  EAGLE WORKS   SAC. CITY
- 7" high, round, cobalt blue, BIMAL.
  F – J.C. PARKER & SON   NEW YORK
- 6¾" high, round, aqua, BIMAL.
  F – TOLENAS SODA SPRINGS
  B – TOLENAS SODA SPRINGS
- 7¼" high, round, green, BIMAL.
  F – PHILADa GLASS WORKS   BURGIN & SONS
- 7¼" high, round, aqua, BIMAL.
  F – DYOTTVILLE GLASS WORKS   PHILAD. [a]
- 7-1/8" high, round, cobalt blue, BIMAL.
  F – OWEN CASEY   EAGLE SODA WORKS
  B – SAC CITY
- 6¾" high, round, aqua, BIMAL.
  F – C. SCHNERR & CO.   SACRAMENTO CAL
  Bm– CAPITAL SODA WORKS

PLATE 6. Left to right. SODAS

- 7" high, 8 sided, cobalt blue, BIMALGP.
  1 – SEITZ & BR<u>O</u>
  2 – EASTON P<u>a</u>
  4 – PREMIUM
  5 – MINERAL
  6 – WATERS
- 7¼" high, 8 sided, green, BIMALGP.
  1 – JOHN S. BAKER
  2 – SODA WATER
  6 – THIS BOTTLE IS NEVER SOLD
- 7¼" high, 10 sided, cobalt blue, BIMALGP.
  1 – W.P.
  3 – KNICKER
  5 – BOCKER
  7 – SODA WATER
  9 – 164. 18TH ST N.Y. 1848
- 7¾" high, round (10 side base) light blue, BIMAL.
  F – HOLDEN'S G.A.
  Bm – CAPITAL SODA WORKS SAC.

Bottom

- 7¼" high, round, green, BIMAL.
  F – WILLIAMS & SEVERANCE SAN FRANCISCO, CAL.
  B – SODA & MINERAL WATERS
- 7" high, round (ten pin), green, BIMALGP.
  F – LUKE BEARD
- 6½" high, round, green, BIMAL.
  F – ROBINSON, WILSON & LEGALLEE
  102 SUDBURY ST. BOSTON
- 7" high, round, green, BIMAL.
  F – E.L. BILLINGS SAC CITY
  B – GEYSER SODA

PLATE 7. Left to right. SARATOGA MINERAL WATERS.

- 7¼" high, round, emerald green, BIMAL.
  F – <u>HATHORN SPRING   SARATOGA NY</u>

- 7¾" high, round light olive amber, BIMAL.
  F – <u>STAR SPRING CO.  *  SARATOGA, N.Y.</u>

- 9½" high, round, emerald green, BIMAL.
  F – <u>EMPIRE SPRING CO   E   SARATOGA N.Y.</u>
  B – <u>EMPIRE WATER</u>

- 9¼" high, round, olive green, BIMAL.
  F – <u>D.A. KNOWLTON   SARATOGA.  N.Y.</u>

- 9¾" high, round, green, BIMAL.
  F – <u>SARATOGA   A   SPRING CO. N.Y.</u>

PLATE 8. Left to right. CONTROVERSIAL.

- 8-3/8" high, round, olive green, BIMAL.
  Around shoulder: <u>DR. J G B SIEGERT & HIJOS</u>
  Bm – <u>DR. SIEGERT   CD BOLIVAR</u>

- 8¾" high, round, amber, BIMAL.
  F   – (canoe)
  To left – <u>H.H. WARNER & CO.</u>
  To right – <u>TIPPECANOE</u>
  Bm – <u>PAT NOV. 20 83   ROCHESTER NY 1</u>

- 9½" high, oval, amber, BIMAL.
  F   – <u>WARNER'S SAFE KIDNEY & LIVER CURE
         ROCHESTER, N.Y.   (safe)</u>
  Bm – <u>WS</u>

- 9¼" high, round, olive green, BIMAL.
  Bm – <u>SAXLEHNERS BITTERQUELLE   HUNYADI JANOS</u>

I tried the Courtland levee again the other day and got a few more things. I just use a short scratcher there and suggest against the use of a shovel; you might get in trouble.

Can someone find out what is made in the Stanford Glass Blowing Laboratory, Inc., 971 Commercial Street, Palo Alto? Just wondering about the possibilities of a field trip.

In one of the Mexican glass factories, Mrs. T. saw the blower blow a nice bottle, attach the pontil, cut off the pipe, and then he gave it a twirl and what had been a bottle turned into a plate. That explains the pontil mark on the bottom of all the Mexican glass dishes.

Geraldine Sheehan reports that the Jarrett Manley's now have another son; this makes three sons for them. With three future bottle diggers, I recommend trying for a bottle washer next time.

Any of you with children have heard about the Purple People Eaters and I guess there must have been such things because Mrs. Sheehan reports that she now has "a purple breast pump...and in perfect shape too." She would like to find out about a three mold green applied lip bottle, "Coca Mariani Paris." Anyone know?

There follows some info sent in by Mrs. Sheehan on the Ehmann Olive Company.

## EHMANN OLIVE COMPANY

"The Ehmann Olive Co. was founded in 1897 in Oakland, Calif.

"In 1897 and 1898 all the processing was done by Mr. Ehmann in the basement of Mr. Bolles home in Oakland. (He was her son-in-law.)

"In 1900 the company built the first unit of what was eventually to become the largest ripe olive packing plant of its time on ground located at 2nd St. and the S.P. tracks in Oroville.

"In 1903 the company built its first olive oil mill and Ehmann Olive Oil was first marketed.

"The Ehmann Olive Oil bottle has a long neck and fluted shoulders may have been used anytime between 1903 and 1927 when that type was discontinued. There were three sizes of the private-mold Ehmann Olive Oil bottles: 5 oz., 10 oz., and 20 oz. liquid capacities. They were manufactured by the Pacific Coast Glass Works in San Francisco and its predecessor. The Pacific Coast Glass Works was later acquired by Ill. Pacific Co., now Owens of Ill."

Thanks, Geraldine.

Am including in these notes Lavine Layton's poem, The Cache of Placer Pete. I'll bet you start scratching through pack rat's nests after you read this.

Just looking through my 1901 Medicology book to give you some info that might be interesting and I believe I found what Mrs. Sheehan's "Coca Mariani" is. In a section, "How to Make Leading Patent Medicines," it shows, "Vin Mariani. Fresh coca leaves, 3 oz.; Port wine, 1 pint. Doze: A wineglass three times a day. Used in acid digestion — fortifies and strengthens the system."

What I was looking for was the recipe for the following items:

"WARNERS SAFE CURE. Powdered salpetre, 2 drachms. Liverwort, 1 oz. Water, sufficient. Alcohol, 2 oz. Glycerine, 1½ oz. Spirits wintergreen, 40 drops."

No wonder it was safe.

"HOP BITTERS. Hops, 4 oz. Orange peel, 2 oz. Dandelion, 2 oz. Buchu, 1 oz. May-apple, ½ oz. Sugar, 16 oz. Alcohol, 16 oz. Water, sufficient."

Be a pretty stiff drink if there was a water shortage.

Those of you that have one of the Wahoo Bitters should know this. Wahoo is the common name for a small shrub, Euonymus atropurpureus, and is listed as a medicinal plant. Also, for Mrs. Sheehan, Coca is a small tree in Peru and Bolivia. The principal constituent of the leaves is cocaine.

I have a 1904 book advertising Peruna. Its title is the "Twelfth Edition of the Ills of Life." I think it mentions about every ill and Peruna was good for all of them. The Peruna Almanac for 1899 had a little different approach. It proclaimed that Peruna would only cure Catarrh but then explained how nearly all ills are catarrh of one sort or another.

Brown's Shakespearian Annual Almanac 1870 is a very nice little book on Dr. O. Phelps Brown's Standard Herbal Remedies. We have a bottle with Dr. O. Phelps Brown on it but that is all that it says. The book advertises The Acacian Balsam, The Restorative Assimilant, The Renovating Pill, The Herbal Ointment, Blood Purifier, The Woodland Balm, and Floral Bloom. J.C.T.

### The Cache of Placer Pete

*Howdy, Friend, Glad you dropped by.*
*I have a little tale that I*
*Would like to pass along to you*
*If you have time to hear me through.*
*You have! Then grab yourself a chair.*
*Take the easy one right here*
*And sit a spell, while I repeat*
*My tale — the Cache of Placer Pete.*

*A century, maybe more, ago,*
*Old Placer Pete and his burro*
*Wandering along a lonely stream*
*Found the riches of his dream.*

*Old Pete, he toiled all summer through*
*His pile of dust and nuggets grew*
*Till grub was gone and winter nigh,*
*Soon, the snow would start to fly.*

*Tarnation now! How could he pack*
*All his pile on Jenney's back?*
*Time for one trip. That was all.*
*Have to cache part of his haul.*

*Now Pete — He was a drinkin' man —*
*Toted his liquor, not in cans*
*But big brown bottles. There they lay*
*Where he had tossed 'em all away.*

*His eye in anxious search around*
*O'er the hard and rocky ground,*
*Fell upon them laying there.*
*Why not? He'd little time to spare!*

He stooped and gathered every one,
   And when his task was finally done,
Every bottle held its load
   Of his previous hard-earned gold.
Into the sand, by the little stream
   Went his treasure, and his dream.
He'd return, come early spring
   Prepared to pack out everything.
Poor Pete! He never came again.
   He went the way of drinking men,
And years passed by. No human feet
   Trod the trail of Placer Pete.
And then, ole' Nature took a hand.
   A spring flood washed across the sand
And all the bottles buried there
   Were left uncovered, brown and bare.
Near the stream, up a little draw,
   A Pack-rat lived, with an itchy paw,
Lookin' for loot, his keen old eye
   Caught the glitter of gold, as he passed by.
You know, I guess, what his kind do?
   Always take back something to
Take the place of what they took?
   Now, Ole' Rat wore an anxious look.
Near his nest a pine tree grew.
   Remembering this, what did he do?
Why, nuts for nuggets, traded he
   From his own well-stocked pantry.
For each nugget he would pack
   Into his nest a nut went back
Into a bottle. He was no cheat
   But he raided the cache of Placer Pete.
A grey-squirrel and his lady-love
   Came to dwell in the pine above
The trade-rat's home. As time went by
   'Twas only right that they multiply.
They did! And how their family grew
   Until there weren't enough nuts to
Go around, and fill the family larder,
   Their search for food grew ever harder.
One day, then, they chanced upon
   Old Pete's bottles, with their brown
Sweet and tender pine nuts there.
   Each squirrel struggled for his share!
Hunger crazed, they forced their heads
   Into the bottles and there they wedged.
No matter how they pulled and pried,
   They stuck! And there they died!
Each bottle held itself a squirrel.
   A breeze danced by, with a merry whirl,
Ruffling the fur on the long grey tails.
   Who can say that Justice fails?

# XVI
## Just a Special Report

Pot luck on June 17th well attended by out-of-towners. Patterson, Kendrick and Saxton from Fallon, Nev.; Williams from Reno; Boynton, Fountain and Quigley from Quincy; Ford and Gruwell from Bishop; Webber from Newcastle; Kosby from San Francisco; Clapp from Yuba City; Handy from Marysville; Herndon from Rackerby; Leach from Stockton; Manley from Bangor; and I may have missed some in the confusion. Sure good to see you people. Many nice displays and a lot of trading and a lot of food. Many thanks to the Neils and the Riebers for putting this on.

GROUP FIELD TRIP. Yep, here we go again. August 4th, 5th and 6th or any parts thereof. Summit City (Meadow Lake) California or where it was. You woodsmen will know how to get there but for most of us it will be Highway 40 to Truckee, North on 89, through Hobart Mills and way on to turn off (westerly) to Weber Lake. As you pass Weber Lake turn south and go along west edge of lake through Lacey Valley and follow signs (I hope) to Meadow Lake. I was there once in a car, roads are fair. Meadow Lake is about T.18N. R.13E. close to Fordyce Lake. There may be better ways to go, I don't know. Send to the U.S. Forest Service and get their Sierraville District Tahoe National Forest Map.

In case some of you feel you can't go because you don't have camping equipment — the wife and I use no tent, sleep on the ground in sleeping bags, cook over an open fire, and enjoy every minute of it. We usually take along bacon, eggs and coffee for breakfast, snacking stuff for lunch, and a steak to broil over the coals for dinner. Incidentally we are usually real thoughtful of those poor people a hundred years from now who will have to settle for collecting beer cans or bottles.

No, we are not apt to find much on a group field trip such as this but who can think of anything nicer than a campfire, after that good steak and coffee, a couple of refreshing drinks, and then listening about the big bottles that got away.

From a trade card copyright 1894: "They won't kick against Pond's Extract because all who use it for burns, colds, catarrh, wounds, earache, lameness, hoarseness, female complaints, piles, boils, scalds, bruises, soreness, sunburn, influenza, itching, sprains, lame back, rheumatism, sore throat, insect stings, varicose veins, headache, old sores, chilblains, toothache, nose bleed, prickly heat, inflamed eyes, for all pain, and for inflammations and hemorrhages, are perfectly satisfied with the beneficient, healing, curing result."

OLD BOTTLES AND GHOST TOWNS by Adele Reed, Chalfant Press, Bishop, April, 1961. About 400 bottles illustrated by our own May Jones. A must book for any western bottle collector. Send $2 plus tax and postage to Adele Reed, Rt. 1, Box 96, Bishop, California.

Watch for August issue of Women's Day at your grocery (Luckies here). Out on July 18. Article on old glass and bottles.

Last Saturday, June 24th, gave speech to Annual Conference of California Historical Societies at Columbia. About what is ABCAC and what connection old bottles and history, title, "History — In a Bottle?" Very well received.  J.C.T.

# XVII
## Summit City Field Trip

September, 1961

Well, here we go again after a summer's recess. Incidentally, where are we going this year? What are our aims and objectives? What do you want to happen? What information would you like in the Pontil? How much time and effort and talent are you ready to spend? That last was a nasty question, wasn't it? But really I have about run out of steam and there will have to be a new President effective January 1, 1962. If desired I will still continue to put out "The Pontil." This in itself really takes a lot of time from beginning to end, but I enjoy it, probably because it satisfies the "ham" in me.

Those of you who missed the trip to Summit City (Meadow Lake) really missed a good trip even if it didn't produce many old bottles. It is a beautiful spot, and we were practically "alone in the woods." Those present were: Harry and Lillian Jorgensen and family, Jim and Barbara Keskeys and family, Fred and Darlene Piggott and guests, Lee and Jackie Scroggins, self and Mrs. T., Willie Vidak and guest, and George Yeager — all from Sacramento. Those from out of town: Bea Boynton and guest from Quincy, Alice Fountain from Quincy, "Toot" and Dorothy Garten from Carson City, Mr. and Mrs. Kissee and son from Red Bluff (Los Molinas), Mr. and Mrs. Lee Martin and guests from Truckee, and Bill and Dorothy Weber and son from Newcastle.

Lee Scroggins came up with the first finds; later Alice Fountain developed a nice mine, but couldn't get through the roots; Harry Jorgensen took over and dug up several including his first "pumpkinseed" flask; later Bill Weber (and/or son) dug up a few including a Roth which I hadn't seen before.

Some real nice finds were made of Indian artifacts: arrowheads, bird points, scrapers, and spear heads. (Did you ever go fishing and have ducks all over?) Lee Martin got one of the prettiest, most perfect points that I have ever seen.

Remember that old song, "I want to cook my coffee in an old tin can"? Well, "Toot" belongs to that school, and it was a sight for sore eyes (and there were a few).

Speaking about songs, have you ever 'Sung Along with Mitch'? Well, our 'Sing Along' by the campfire Saturday night surely included every song "Mitch" has ever sung, although I did hear one complaint (that I would listen to) the next morning about one we had missed and the person had stayed awake listening for it.

Who poured their dishwater all over my sleeping bag in the dark???

Ten of us walked clear around the lake in search of the houses reputed to have been over there. It must have been an ill repute; we didn't find any houses. Someone did find all the fragments of a Plantation Bitters. I did find part of an old oar that probably was used to cross the lake, and after walking around I would have used a boat myself.

Had a nice letter from Adele Reed thanking me for the bit I put in the last Pontil on her book. We are all invited to stop and see their bottle house anytime we are in Bishop.

Had a nice letter from Jerry McMullen, San Diego Historical Society, about my speech at Columbia. Quoting his last paragraph..."Again, it was a wonderful talk, although I almost had a stroke when you said that you were going to wind up by reading to the audience the immortal lines of 'Lydia Pinkham.' I was just on the point of jumping up and screaming, 'You wouldn't dare!'."

Just received a letter from the San Joaquin County Historical Society asking me to give this same talk for them in October. Bottle Collecting is on the way up. Incidentally, Bea, one of their members that heard me and recommended me is a Miss Boynton. Relation?

Nice letter from Bea Boynton giving us this bit of information from the San Francisco Chronicle, 7-23-61. "A key unit in the Jackson Square development is the iron-shuttered Hotaling Building, a one-time distillery headquarters, which survived the fire of 1906 and was thereupon immortalized by poet Charley Field:

*'If, as they say, God spanked the town*
*For being over-frisky,*
*Why did he burn the churches down*
*And spare Hotaling's whiskey?'"*

How many of you have a Hotaling's Whiskey? Bea does.

Tom Brown gave me a clipping from the "100 Years Ago" section of the Sacramento Bee, dated 6-29-61: "For a long time there has been no Napa soda in the market. Last night a large supply arrived in this city for the agent, Phil Cuduc, who has a lease of the springs which produce this delicious natural beverage, so grateful in warm weather."

Have practically finished my book, "Bottles Up." A little more to add to Chapter 13 and a little polish on Chapter 16, and it is done. Had hoped to get Century House to publish, but Freeman is not interested. He thinks it should cover the entire field, not just the later bottles that we are finding out here. It would sure be a big book if it did. Personally, I feel there are already good books and will be more on the real old and fancy things. I had hoped for a nice hard-cover book with 12 color plates and many black and white pictures. If I don't find an interested publisher, I will have to go to a "vanity" publisher who will do anything you pay for. In this case, the plates, pictures and hard cover will have to go. Anyone have a rich aunt in the publishing game?

I have a little advertising pin cushion that says, "Ely's Cream Balm applied into the nostrils is quickly absorbed. Soothes and Heals. Quickly gives relief. Positively cures Catarrh, Cold in head and Hay-fever." I had thought it was a cosmetic.

In a little catalog I have, "Nature's Herbal Remedies," I find that Damiana is a Mexican Herb. So now we know that our *Damiana Bitters* (Plate # 2 ) has Damiana in them. In Ensenada this summer we saw a recipe for a mixed drink that called for 1 oz. of Damiana.

I now have a beautiful little booklet on *Dr. Siegert's* Angostura Bitters (Plate # 8 ). This has several testimonials dated in the early 1870's, testifying to its value for many ailments. It has more to say on this score than on the other use. This bitters was first made in 1830.

*J.C.T.*

# XVIII
## Did You Ever Taste Zedoary?

October, 1961

THIS AND THAT — *J.C.T.*

I sent east and purchased five old 5-gallon blown glass demijons. In lots of five they were only $3.50 each but the freight brought the cost of each up to $7.00. Bea Boynton got one of these and asked by letter if they could be the ones mentioned in McKearens. Yes, Bea, they are. Quoting from the ad, "Purchased 101 years ago by Dr. Welch, founder of Welch Grape Juice Com., from Whitewall Tatum Co., Milleville, N.J." April 1960 ad.

Jackie and Lee Scroggins made a wonderful buy from the east. Sight unseen they sent off for and got twelve *case bottles* (Plate # 9 ) in the original old case. These are beautiful old freeblown bottles shaped like the larger Hoboken bottles but with no writing on them and with pontil scars. No two are alike but they are all beautiful.

Mrs. T. and I drove out to Dixon to contact a glass blower and see if we could get him for one of our meetings. He works and lives there and is willing to give us a talk for $10 or a talk and demonstration for $25. The Scroggins and Garth Patterson had told us about him. Actually he is a lampworker not a glass blower. He blows things from pyrex glass tubes which he melts over a torch (lamp). He gave us quite a little demonstration and I believe it would be worth the money to have him if we can get the city's approval for the use of the necessary equipment in the Center.

I read something the other day that clears up the nickname of a famous western bottle collector that has puzzled me for a long time. I am sure that many others of you will be glad to know this also. An Indian petitioned a judge of a Nevada court to give him a shorter name. "What is your name now?" asked the Judge. "Chief Screeching Train Whistle," the Indian replied. "And what do you want to change it to?" the Judge asked. "Toot," replied the Indian. — how goes it over on the Nevada bottle reservation, Chief?

Sammy Kissee of Los Molinas sent in sketches and questions on four bottles. The nice shaped one reading "A. Durand & Fils Hule D'Salad Bordeaux" is French and translates to "A. Durand & Sons Salad Oil Bordeaux." The similarly shaped one with no writing was probably Olive Oil. Your South Carolina Dispensary bottle is probably a bottle from the Civil War. We have one very similar in shape and size that reads, "U.S. Hospital Department." Your Pacific Congress Water is the familiar old soda water bottle. I believe Congress Springs was a famous old mineral water springs back east and probably this western company tried to borrow a little of the name.

We now have members in Oregon and Arizona as well as California and Nevada. Someday we may have to change the ABCAC to ABCAA.

Gave my bottle speech to the San Joaquin County Historical Ass'n. last Monday night in Lodi. Fairly well received, but not as well as it had been at State Conference in Columbia. This was their annual dinner meeting and it was held in the First Methodist Church. To me, parts of my talk just were not exactly at home in church and this probably affected my delivery. Oh well, a rose is a rose is a rose.

The Scroggins have a book that I am going to buy as soon as I can get to the right store. It is wonderful and a must for anyone interested in the "patent" medicines. "One For A Man, Two For A Horse" by Gerald Carson and published by Doubleday & Company, Inc. Some of you will remember a list of recommended books I had in the notes a long time back which included "The Country Store" by this same author. This new book is an elaboration of Chapter 11 of the old book. The new book is very well done and is both informative and humorous and is full of pictures of the old advertising.

Speaking about books, Doubleday and Company, Inc. have asked to see my manuscript. I have it all ready to mail as soon as three little sketches of necks and stoppers are completed. From the letters I have had, I know many of you are glad to hear this. Incidentally, I want to thank all of you for the encouragement you have given me and the confidence you seem to have in my ability. I am encouraged by Doubleday's offer, but am fully aware that they must read many manuscripts for every one they publish. Keep your fingers crossed.

Hurry, hurry, hurry! Go out and buy the November issue of The American Home Magazine. Among other interesting collections shown and described is a part of Charles Gardner's wonderful bottle collection. This will make you drool.

We have a champagne type old bottle with a blob glass seal on the shoulder reading "Fratelli Branca." An old trade card we have indicates that this shape bottle could have been their Vieux Cognac. Another trade card advertises an old specialty of Fratelli Branca to be "Fernet-Branca" and claims it to be Italy's best bitters. I found a bottle of this the other day while browsing in a liquor store and bought it for the advertising and also to taste. Holy smokes! If this isn't Italy's best bitters, it is surely their bitterest. It may be good for Manhattans, I hope so. It is advertised as Italy's famous bitter stimulant to the appetite. (I couldn't taste anything else for two hours.) From the advertising, "Contains alcohol by volume, 39%, aloes, cinchona bark, gentian, rhubarb, zedoary, calumba, agaric, galangal, bryonia, calamus, angelica, myrrh, chamomile and peppermint." I am sure all that I tasted was the zedoary but it may have been the agaric. This company was established in 1845.

Calvert Distillers Company has just put out a limited edition series of four flasks patterned after the old historical flasks and with no increase in price. These are fifths and are Courage, Liberty, Friendship and Plenty. We have Liberty; it is in a nice light green. The Liberty side has an eagle while the reverse shows the Flag and cannon. The nasty words are on the bottom and are small. The stopper is a hollow glass ball which is open into the bottle. These bottles are nice and I predict that they will become collectors' items in just a few years. Two ounces of the product in a tall glass filled with ice and water is very good too.

J.C.T.

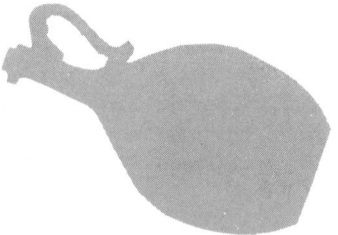

## XIX
### Enter C. B. Gardner

November, 1961

*11-25-61*

*'Twas just one month before Christmas*
  *When all through the house,*
*There were bottles and bottles — and even my spouse*
  *Was thinking of bottles — preparing a speech,*
*Some club, dumb on bottles, asked her to teach.*
*I was cut to the quick, the reason you'll see*
  *They wanted my wife, they didn't want me!*
*She had helped me out once, I'd been called out of town*
  *And now her fame's up while mine's fallen down.*
*So fame never lasts and your public is fickle*
  *The truth twists you up like your mouth with a pickle.*
*But I'll rise above this and 'fore I fade out of sight —*
  *Merry Christmas to all and to all a good night.*

    Pardon me, Lavine, but I just have to use my corny poetry once in a while. How about that? This lady called me and explained very carefully how they wanted Mrs. T., not me. Just kidding, of course, because I know her "bottle arrangements" type of presentation is very good and I am proud of her.

    At our November meeting Jackie Scroggins acted as secretary — here is the gist of her notes... The mineral show (Golden Harvest of Gems) held on November 5 and 6 was very successful. Dealers and visitors were here from all over the state. ABCAC won a special display ribbon for our two cases of bottles and the Mineral Society extended their thanks for our display. We had one miscellaneous case and one of pickles, hot sauces, foods, etc.

    Mr. T. asked for volunteers for the Historical Show which will be our second annual "Journey Into the Past" and to be held at the Garden and Arts Center the first weekend in February, 1962.

    Everyone was asked to start planning their display. February will be here before you know it. Grace Neil asked if we could have arranging lesson at meeting before show. All other ladies agreed. Mrs. T. will try to arrange.

    Letter read from Adele Reed, Bishop, asking Mr. T's opinion on her writing another book to be a price guide on western bottles. Members present seemed to favor idea if prices were realistic.

THIS AND THAT — *J.C.T.*

Thanks, Jackie.

    George Rieber brought some information for those of you with any Justin Gates bottles. Came to California at age of 21 in 1849, one of the first graduate chemists to arrive. He brought a large load of medical supplies and opened an apothecary shop in Sacramento. Soon had a thriving business at 64 K Street and sent for his two brothers from the east. He conceived the idea of using four horse wagons as traveling drugstores accompanied by capable apothecaries. These traveled to the back woods, gold camps and towns. By 1861, the firm was listed as importers, wholesale and retail dealers in drugs, medicines, chemicals, etc.

Floyd Cooper of Anderson asks for information on Wait's Bitters and *Kilmer's Swamp Root* (Plate # 4 ) and also advises he has Hostetter's to trade for other bitters.

My 1908 Swamp Root Almanac has this to say — "Hay un consuelo en el saber, tan amenudo expresado, que la Swamp Root (raiz de pantano) del Dr. Kilmer, en gran remedio para los —" and then lists most ailments. This advertises it as a "Remedy" guaranteed under the Pure Food and Drug Act and containing 9% alcohol. My 1906 Almanac advertises it as a "Cure" and states that it cures acute and chronic kidney, liver, bladder and urinary disorders.

Remember — most "cures" changed to "remedies" on 7/1/06.

In referring to my manuscript, I find I was able to date the start of Swamp Root back to about 1885.

My book shows that Ed Hughes has a Wait's Kidney and Liver Bitters and that I have a Wait's Wild Cherry Tonic. The Scroggins have the bitters with a paper label. It was made by George Z. Wait, Wholesale and Retail Druggists, 531 J Street, Sacramento.

By the way, Doubleday acknowledged receipt of my manuscript a few weeks ago and said I would hear from them later. I am afraid the book may be about two years ahead of the spread of the hobby as we practice it — but maybe no news is good news.

Mrs. Hillman, San Francisco, sent us a short article with pictures from the S.F. Sunday Chronicle Bonanza, 11/12/61, "Napa Soda Springs Is Now Crumbling Into Ruins." It tells us that these were an Elite California Spa during the 80's and 90's, and that they were an extravagant example of Victorian gingerbread and of builder Colonel J.P. Jackson's eclectic taste. Most of these beautiful old buildings were destroyed by fire in 1941. Going back to my book, I find, "This water has been on the market since 1860, the plant at present" (1913) "having a capacity of 1000 dozen splits per day."

A friend brought me an item from the Redding Record — Searchlight, 11/15/61. "Tread gently in Trinidad lest you ruin an artifact." It tells of the many old things including bottles that Merlin McGinnis is finding in that area. It specifically mentions the Posey Gulch area near Lewiston. He has now bought a metal detector to help them in their search. He intimates it is the perfect family hobby and I sure agree with him.

An interesting book I have been reading, "The Eternal Search" by Richard Mathison, states that one of the earliest and most famous of the patent medicines was Dr. Bateman's Pectoral Drops, first sold in 1726. Anyone have it or the Ascension flask? The main ingredients were opium and alcohol seasoned with camphor and anise.

This book also tells that the medicine shows reached their zenith between 1880 and 1895. Top among these was The Great Kickapoo Indian Medicine Company which was founded in 1881. One of the founders of Kickapoo Indian Oil was John Healy who had previously made and peddled his King of Pain.

Sent off an order for a flask to Charles B. Gardner and included the October Pontil. Today we received a very nice letter from him acknowledging the order and thanking us for the notes. Yes, Mr. Gardner, I would like very much to take advantage of your offer to let me show our group the slides you mention and also any other pictures or material on bottles. We will be glad to pay any expenses involved. Ours is a group eager to learn and anything you send will be greatly appreciated.

Mr. Gardner advises that my informant was in error and that Mrs. Myrtle Clevenger is carrying on the business; also that Congress Springs was at Saratoga, N.Y.; also that "Thompson once offered me what he called a cocktail from bitters which I refused as I valued my life." After my Fernet Branca tasting, I think Mr. G. is a smart man.

Here is the answer to a bottle collector's dream and I quote from Mr. G.'s letter, "Invite your group to stop in if they come east and I can assure them of a real treat."

Thank you, Mr. Gardner. If you get out this way, look us up — we can't tell you or show you much, but you might enjoy meeting a bunch of eager western bottle diggers. *J.C.T.*

## XX
## From 17 People to 130 Families

December, 1961

Out of the original 17 people that got together to form this club, five were present tonight: Barbara Keskeys, Jackie and Lee Scroggins and John and Edith Tibbitts.

A very nice Certificate of Appreciation was shown that was given to us by the Mineral society for our display in their show.

Mr. T. read a letter from the Tylers in El Dorado County asking about what would be involved in a group up there forming a club, whether they should be a chapter of our organization or be independent. Mr. T. also had just received a call from Ned Kendricks, Fallon, Nevada, asking the same question.

There followed some discussion on by-laws, being a parent organization, etc., etc.

Mr. T. brought up for discussion the fact that he felt the dues were too high for associate members. He felt they should be reduced to more nearly only the costs involved in the Pontil. Tom Neil made the motion which was seconded and carried: Dues for associates to be $2 a year (half price) letting the members themselves decide whether they were Associates or Regular.

Willi Vidak reported she had asked the Garden Center to purchase three books, the "Two McKearins" and "One For a Man, Two For a Horse." She explained how the Center's Library operates and told of all the wonderful books already available to us. Books may be borrowed at a meeting in one month and returned at the meeting the following month.

Mr. T. gave very sincere thanks to all who had worked with him the last two years and then conducted a simple installation of the new officers.

For a program, the club must thank Mrs. T. for bringing her bottles and materials and giving her "Bottle Arranging" talk. It was very good, even the men enjoyed it. *J.S.*

THIS AND THAT — *J.C.T.*

Have we made any progress in two years? Not all I had hoped for, but — We advanced from 17 *people* to 130 *families*. The best bottle anyone had then was a Warner's Safe. Most of us didn't know a pontil mark from a belly-button, nor how to tell a machine produced bottle. We had no idea what or how many bottles there were nor where to see another collector. Most of us didn't know another collector and were beginning to think we were crazy. We knew none of the historical facts about the companies behind our bottles. Bottles could be found only in "junk" stores — now they are in "Antique" Shops. Then we met in homes but are now a member club of the elite Garden and Art Center. And so on —.

I feel we have come a long way and are now in a good position to become the parent organization of a growing nationwide group of clubs. This hobby, as we practice it, has grown and spread tremendously in just two years and probably 90% of the growth has been from brand new, eager, bottlers. As you know, after one finds about two bottles, they are hooked and there is no reason to think we have a corner on this in this area. We have already spread to three other states and it can spread and spread.

Editorially speaking, I feel we should become a parent club of a *simple* organization for any and all clubs that will spring up. We owe this to them and everyone will gain by it. This should be nothing more than having them accept our basic objectives and agreeing to exchange club notes with all other clubs. I feel the best way to ruin our club or a chance for a group of clubs, would be to get all bound up with a Constitution, complex By-Laws, and Robert's Rules of Order.

My last act before turning the gavel over to Lee the other night was to make Charles B. Gardner a permanent honorary member of ABCAC. This doesn't mean much, Mr. Gardner, except that we appreciate your friendly letters and want to send you the "Pontil" each month. I hope you continue to enjoy them.

Quoting from my last letter from Mr. G. — "tell the lady that bought the Fislerville (not Fisherville) Jenny that she can easily distinguish the fake as the smoke coming out of the chimney is simply outlined, where in the original the smoke is a glob or raised. The original is shorter and the neck tapers." "...as Homer Eaton Keyes former Editor of Antiques once said, 'Gardner, I am glad to find one of these damn fool collectors who appreciate a full bottle as well as an empty one' and this may appeal to visiting bottle collectors as I have an old bar for the purpose of entertaining."

When do we leave, Toot?

In his letter, Mr. G. also tells of the pictures and slides he is sending for our next meeting. I have received these *and you had better be at the next meeting, January 2, 1962.* There are 22 color slides we will show on the big screen, 18 color pictures, and 39 black and white.

A friend brought me a bottle found during some remodeling at Folsom Prison. It's a clear fifth (will probably turn) and in addition to a paper label it had a cloth label reading, "We promise to pay $1.00 for 12 of these Coupons — Jas. E. Pepper and Co." Also, "$5500 Premium Notice — We will pay to the person returning during the year 1898 The Greatest Number $2500 — To the Second $1500 —" etc. "Jas. E. Pepper and Co. Distillers, Lexington, Ky., U.S.A."

Bet this was the start of "green stamps." Think how happy you could keep the little lady by bringing her home one of these coupons each day. Anyone have Jas. E. Pepper in the glass?

The Chalfant Press, Bishop, sent me a copy of May Jones' book,

PLATE 9. Left to right. CASE BOTTLES.

- 9″ high, case, light olive amber, FB.
  A beautiful old specimen but no apparent pontil.
- 9-5/8″ high, case, green, ABM.
  F – <u>AVAN HOBOKEN & C<sup>O</sup> ROTTERDAM</u>
  B – <u>AVAN HOBOKEN & C<sup>O</sup> ROTTERDAM</u>
  Inside circular ring on corner shoulder: <u>AVH</u>
- 10″ high, case, light olive green, FBOP.
  Another beautiful old specimen but with definite open pontil.
  Came in an old case chest with eleven others but no two alike.
- 10¾″ high, case, amber green, BIMAL.
  F – <u>AVAN HOBOKEN & C<sup>O</sup> ROTTERDAM</u>
  B – <u>AVAN HOBOKEN & C<sup>O</sup> ROTTERDAM</u>
  Blob seal on corner shoulder: <u>AVH</u>

  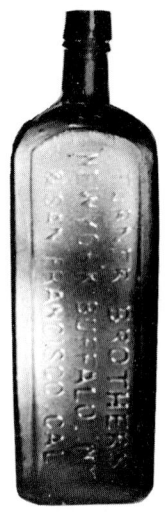 

PLATE 10. Left to right. MISCELLANEOUS.

- 9¾" high, square, light olive amber, BIMAL.
  F – AROMATIC SCHNAPPS
  B – UDOLPHO WOLFE'S
  R – SCHIEDAM

- 10" high, square semi cabin, amber, BIMAL.
  F – PERRINE'S (large apple) GINGER (on panel)
      GINGER (on shoulder)
  L – APPLE (on shoulder)
  B – PERRINE'S
  R – PHIL.ᵃ

- 10" high, square, olive green, BIMAL.
  F – TURNER BROTHERS
      NEW YORK, BUFFALO, .N Y.
      & SAN FRANCISCO. CAL.

- 9½" high, square, amber, BIMAL.
  F – OLD LONDON DOCK
  L – GIN
  R – A.M.BININGER & CO.
      NO. 19 BROAD Sᵗ    N.Y.

PLATE 11. Left to right. WHISKIES.

- 10" high, round, amber, BIMAL.
  F – <u>CROWN DISTILLERIES COMPANY</u> (crown & monogram w/CDCo)
  Bm – <u>PCGW</u>

- 7¾" high, barrel, amber, BIMALOP.
  Around top: <u>DISTILLED IN 1848</u>
  In center around bung: <u>OLD KENTUCKY BOURBON 1849 RESERVE</u>
  Around bottom: <u>A.M. BININGER & CO. 19 BROAD ST. N.Y.</u>

- 4½" high, round, amber, BIMAL.
  F – <u>CROWN DISTILLERIES COMPANY</u> (crown & monogram w/CDCo)
  Bm – <u>PCGW</u>

- 4" high, pumpkin seed (picnic) flask, amber, BIMAL.
  F – <u>PAP'S PICNIC'S</u> (inside circular wreath design)
  Bm – <u>S.C. CO.</u>

PLATE 12. Left to right. FOODS.

- 11¼" high, 2¼" mouth, square cathedral, aqua, BIMAL.
  Gothic arches on 4 sides, 3 with diamond pane windows, one plain for label. Probably for pickles or chutney.

- 8½" high, square cathedral, aqua, BIMALOP.
  Gothic arches on all four sides both upper & lower. A peppersauce.

- 8¾" high, 6 sided cathedral, aqua, BIMALOP.
  Gothic arches on all 6 sides both upper & lower. A peppersauce.

- 8" high, 6 sided ridgy, green, BIMAL.
  13 horizontal rings all around all 6 sides.
  Bm — PATENTED ERD & Co FEB 74.

- 6-5/8" high, rect. taper, green, BIMAL.
  Fluted corners, 12 vertical ridges in lower half of neck. A caper.

- 8-5/8" high, rect., green, BIMAL.
  Fluted corners. Possibly a caper.

"Bottle Trails." May is the one who did the illustrations for Adele Reed's book. May's book gives some interesting historical information on the companies behind a limited number of our bottles. You can get this book directly from the Chalfant Press, but no price was given me in or out of the book.

The program committee, Elmer Lester and Associates, have asked everyone to bring a display of Patent Medicines to the January 2nd meeting so I will tell you about a few of the old trade cards we have on medicines.

Ayer's Ague Cure was a purely vegetable bitter and tonic, warranted a cure for Fever, Ague and all disorders peculiar to malarious, marshy and miasmatic districts.

Ayer's Sarsaparilla:
> Sarsaparilla was the name by which this Extract
> gained its fame
> Oh happy day she cried for lo! The pimples
> soon began to go
> And now the fairest of the fair, She lives
> to bless the name of Ayer.

Barry's Triopherous established 1801 guaranteed to restore hair to bald heads and to make it grow thick, long and soft.

Indulgence in Forbidden Fruit produces a sure crop of colic, cramps and cholera morbus. Fortunately the mischief is repaired by Perry Davis Pain Killer.

Dr. Kilmer's Female Remedy. Give it to your weak and delicate daughters. Not a drop of impure blood can escape its healing and purifying influence.

Maltine is a pure extract of malted barley, wheat and oats and was invaluable in securing sound and healthy digestion.

Minard's Linament — The King of Pain. 25¢ per bottle.

St. Jacobs Oil, the Great German Remedy, It Conquers Pain.

Wistar's Balsam of Wild Cherry for Coughs and all Lung Diseases. Consumption Can Be Cured.

About time for Christmas Dinner so had better close these notes.

Feliz Navidad y Ano Nuevo Prospero — *J.C.T. & E.E.T.*

P.S. Lee just called me and said that Mr. Earl Barnett of the Arrangers Guild will be with us at the January 2nd meeting to give us the lowdown on Arrangements with Bottles. This will be just in time to help us for the February Show.

# XXI
## Some Information Out of Harper's Weekly, 1865-66

January, 1962

### THIS AND THAT — *J.C.T.*

This was "compliment the editor" month from the out-of-towners. I had some real nice letters and thank each of you for those kind words and sort of makes it worthwhile. Yes, t does take a lot of time. I probably

49

average 12 to 13 hours an issue and Mrs. T. adds another 2 or 3.

Mrs. Ruth Paul — your $2.50 purchase is a *Moses' Poland Water* (Plate #15) bottle. One with screw top is pictured on page 111 and 124 of Maust's Bottle and Glass Handbook. The originals held the medicinal waters from Poland Springs. Maust states that originals are hard to find and that many reproductions have been made.

Adele Reed advises she has given up the price guide idea — too big a task with so much variation in prices from here to there. I don't blame her for not taking this on yet.

From the Kreiss':
1. James E. Pepper in the glass shows Carroll & Carroll as agents. 1905-06 San Mateo Co. Dir. shows them at 120 Front St., S.F.
2. Same directory shows: Cartan, McCarthy, 312 Sacramento St.; F. Chivalier, 9 Beach St.; E.A. Fargo, 316 Front St.; Hey, Graurholz (Davy Crockett), 224 Front St.; Hildebrant, Posner, 120 Market St.; Hilbert Bros., 101 Powell St.; Jesse Moore-Hunt, 202 Davis St.; Shea-Bocqueraz, 525 Market; Hotalings, 429 Jackson St. — all S.F.
3. 1902 phone book shows the Pacific Coast Glassworks at 7th and Irwin.
4. Also four very nice drawings. I will try to figure out how to reproduce these — if not practical, I will have one of them traced each month. They are very nice.

Neva Markham, 1386 Jeffries St., Anderson, invites members to drop in and see her collection whenever in that area. Seems everyone goes to see Ted Jones (not a member) who has a fabulous collection. She reports she was thrilled with her latest find when she dug out a California Fig and Herb Bitters. This is different than the one in Adele's book. I would have been thrilled too.

I've got to get back to some of those names given us by the Kreiss'.

*Hey — Graurholz*
*Shea — Bocqueraz*
*Wie treu sind deine blater*
*Du grunst nich nur zur zummerzeit*
*Mein auch in winter wen es schniet*
*Hey — Graurholz*
*Shea — Bocqueraz*
*Could warm you up forever.*

Try it to Oh Maryland, or Tannenbaum, and forgive the 30 years I've spent forgetting the one year of German I learned.

Mrs. Joe Green dropped by to show me a Jos. E. Pepper she has and brought along two bound years of Harpers Weekly, 1865 and 1866. These she left for us to peruse and I will have some items in these notes from them.

Grace Neil reports digging up a *Tamale bottle* (Plate #16) without a scratch. This rates right along with the perfect Pretzel bottle Mrs. T. dug up. These oddities are certainly unique to dig up. Leave it to the gals to dig up food one way or another.

Talking about digging things up...? etc. A couple of Sundays ago Mrs. T. and I went over to the current local bonanza, the Bottle Mine by the zoo. This place is between a housing project (completed), a RR track, a highway, and Land Park Zoo. A fair size house lot would cover the whole area. We saw there the darndest bunch of nondescript, dirty crazy people down in holes you ever did see. Closer inspection revealed the Husons (2), the fairer Rieber (1), the Neils (5), fair Miller (1), fair Knapp (1), the Gaylords (3), the Duncans (5), Winters (2), Kellys (2), and (sorry) a gentleman and his son I just couldn't place. The Tibbitt's (2) poked around a bit and left — guess we got used to the wide open spaces when we were desert rats.

The day before this Lou and Betty Denchfield came up with about 40 bottles there including a Warner's Safe and many nice Sodas.

Wonder if the RR track has caved in yet? This old dump is near the old site of Sutterville and could produce some really old bottles.

I thanked Mr. Gardner in a letter for his slides and pictures but am sure all of you that saw them want to see this club-expression of thanks in the notes — so here they are, Mr. G. Everyone, and it was one of our largest meetings, really enjoyed seeing your wonderful collection.

The following are bottled products which I found advertised in Mrs. Green's Harpers Weeklies:

1-21-65, Dr. O. Phelps Brown, Jersey City — Treatise on sure cure for Dyspepsia and Fits.

2-4-65, "Twelve years ago *Hostetter's Stomach Bitters* (Plate # 3 ) was struggling into notice..."

9-9-65, "Fragrant Sozodont for the Teeth."

9-30-65, "Greenbacks are good — Robacks are Better." Pictures the barrel bottle with a label reading in part, "Dr. C.W. Roback's Unrivalled Stomack Bitters." Bottle has six rings below label and seven above.

11-25-65, Dr. Wm. Hall's Balsam for the Lungs, A.L. Scovill & Co.

12-30-65, "Burnett's Cocoaine — for embellishing and strengthening the hair — ."

12-30-65, "S-T-1860-X. *Drake's Plantation Bitters*" (Plate # 2 ). Drake & Co., New York. Hey bottlers, what do you know, the S, T, & X must be an abbreviation for St. Croix. "They are made of pure St. Croix Rum..."

12-15-66, "Constitution Life Syrup has produced a Revolution in Medicine."

Well, that was a little over four hours searching without too much results of interest to bottlers. Evidently this time was before the hey-day of the patent medicines. I have seen much more profuse advertising in the 80's and 90's. Two items that did have profuse advertising in '65 and '66 were pens (points) and preparations to *grow* whiskers. Don't times change.

Received another real nice letter from Mr. G. today. Advised he had answered George Reiber's letter asking about fakes (from the new program "question bottle").

Quoting Mr. G.'s last paragraph, "In the line of promotion. If you think it a good idea, I can send along applications (to join ABCAC) in my correspondence to collectors, for even if they are not in California, the Pontil will repay them."

I like this thought of spreading out and finding out what's going on all over the country. Discussed this with our President and he does too. He asked me to take care of it. So — I will fix up an information sheet for this year's show the same as we did last year. This time I will make it a little more general and include an application blank. This we will give out at the show, at meetings, give to potential members, use as replies to letters of inquiry, and send a supply to Mr. Gardner.

Have another nice poem from Lavine Layton. Will get it in the next issue. Too much already this issue.

Mrs. T. and I are going to Placerville this Friday to do what we can to help them regarding a club there. Our president tells me that Lou Denchfield has a committee meeting scheduled to draft our Constitution, By-Laws, other clubs relationships, etc. This will be good — just hope it is kept simple and practical.                                         *J.C.T.*

## XXII
### Change Name to
### Antique Bottle Collectors Association
### or ABCA

THE PONTIL

ABCA                                                                February 25, 1962

ANTIQUE BOTTLE COLLECTOR'S ASSOCIATION

Here are the proposed Constitution and By-Laws for our organization. This will be discussed and voted on at the meeting on 3/6/62.

Out-of-towners are invited to submit comments to the President, Lee Scroggin, 6737 51st St., Sacramento 24, Calif.

Lou Denchfield, his committee, and our President are to be complimented for a difficult job well done.

You can blame me for the Article on Associate Clubs.

A couple of quotes from a C.B. Gardner letter: "By the way the reproduction Poland Spring Water bottles or Moses as they are called all are marked Facsimile. The one with the threaded mouth was put out right after prohibition filled with gin with a ball stopper. Just checked mine and it has the ball stopper but no threads and come to think of it I never saw an old one with a threaded mouth and the old ones were always the large size. There is an unusually large one with about the same figure but no lettering. Must have been made for lamp bases.

"Helen McKearin sent back three pictures of bitters out of the twelve I sent her to try to get clearer pictures so I have to go to work on these. At least there will be some bitters in the new book.

"You are a very enthusiastic group and seem to function smoothly. Believe me if I was nearer I would be in the thick of it."

Note: Constitution and By-Laws not included in "Chips."

*J. C. Tibbitts, Editor*

# XXIII
## Resolutions of a Bottle Bug
### by
### Lavine Layton

March, 1962

For the first time in over two years we had a new face behind the fist pounding the gavel — and what a treat to look upon Lee's youthful, handsome face. (I have to get even some way!) Anyway, seriously, we are pleased to have someone of Lee's enthusiasm and capabilities guiding the club activities.

Willi Vidak, club librarian, announced that the books we requested the Garden and Art Center to buy for us, had arrived. We now have available for our use Helen McKearin's "American Glass" and Gerald Carson's "One For A Man and Two For A Horse." In order that everyone may use, or at least see these books, four people may sign up for each book for a month, the first signee to pass it along to the next on the list, the last on the list being responsible for returning it to the Club the following meeting. Incidentally, those of you who tried unsuccessfully to purchase McKearin's "American Glass" will be interested to know that this is a January 1962 edition.

A committee composed of Joe Kelley, Chairman, Elmer Lester, Harriet Reiber, Gene Stodgill and George Yeager, was appointed to contact the Redevelopment Agency to gain permission for club members to dig for bottles in the area, to offer our assistance in the preservation of old bottles from this section, not only for individual collectors but also for the proposed State Historical Museum, and to extend an invitation to them to attend our meetings to see the aims and purposes of the Club.

The display for this month was Redevelopment finds.

Mr. Ed Combatalade gave us an amusing informative speech and displayed his snuff bottle collection.

The program for April will be Mrs. DeWitt Nelson who will display and discuss pressed glass. *E.E.T. protem*

### THIS AND THAT — *J.C.T.*

At the party after the show on Saturday night, we got a preview showing of the museum room at the Firehouse 3. Many nice bottles up there. Then we were taken downstairs to a little banquet room where I got the surprise of my life! Words failed me then — and still do — so I will revert to verse.

> *"A Gift From All Of Us"* it said on the card.
>   And I tried to thank you, but words came too hard.
> It seems my emotions all came into play
>   But then real deep feelings seem to stick in their way.
> The gift was a bottle, a flask, u G-one-27
>   A Washington Eagle — to me straight from heaven.
> But it wasn't the bottle that tied me up so,
>   'Twas just what it meant; this, I want YOU to know.

Well, in contrast to last year, we had real lousy weather the weekend of our show. Even with "dangerous to drive in" cold fog we had over 3000 people attend. Our part of the show was better than last year and the committee and exhibitors deserve a real pat on the back. Even with the terrible weather we had six members from Fallon, Nev., three from Reno, Nev., two from Carson City, Nev., one from Bishop, four from Quincy, one from Fort Bragg, three from San Francisco, two from Oroville that I saw and still remember.

Someone at our house over the show weekend told us that Bekins Brass Polish will take the stain off glass. Believe it is a Chinese product as it was sold here only at May Gim's or Fong's.

Hey, did you notice who signed the notes above? That's my wife and she "got even" but then I think Jackie is cute, too. Look Lee, get another "spare" secretary. I share my house, car, kids, dog, table and bed with her but must I share the Pontil, too?

We visited the Godfrey's out of Grass Valley today. A real nice collection of bottles they have, but listen to this: They have 400 acres of land in that gold rush country, a trout stream right through it, old mine shafts here and there. They have gotten some real nice bottles right on their own property and he even has a bulldozer of his own with which he has turned up some finds. Real rough, isn't it, you city slickers? By the way, these good country folk got the Travelers Bitters from Mr. Gardner.

The March issue of the Spinning Wheel magazine has an article on poison bottles. Those of you who do not take the Saturday Evening Post better find a 3/10/62 issue and look on page 66. Those 18th Century "melon" flasks will make your mouth water!

Which reminds me ... at the Placerville meeting which we attended, we met a lady bottler who got started with the hobby from finding old bottles while skindiving in some of the Sierra Lakes. Is going to try Meadow Lake this summer. That could be real good. The group in Placerville did not decide that night whether to form a local club or what. Now that they have our Constitution and By-Laws, maybe they have decided.

Had a nice letter from Alice Osborne, Secretary of the new "Shasta Antique Bottle Collectors." She wanted our Constitution and By-Laws and to know if they can affiliate with us. She personally feels that all new clubs should affiliate with us.

Grace Kendricks of Fallon sent me the notes from the third and fourth meetings of the Fallon Bottle Club. They, too, want to know about affiliation. Some material in these notes that I may use now or later.

Carol Farrell of Rosemead writes that they have the start of an associate club down there. Present roster of 25 and believes it will grow like Topsy. In the Los Angeles area it sure could. They call themselves the San Gabriel Valley Bottle Collectors. They like the way we are organized and want to follow suit.

Well, here are four new clubs that want to pattern themselves after us and affiliate in some way. Where will this lead to, as the hobby continues to spread, as it is bound to? Just to give you an idea of how the club is growing, here is a resume of the new Addressograph plates I have to have made up to mail this Pontil: 3 in Sacramento area, 25 in other California locations, 2 in Wyoming, 1 in Michigan, 3 in Florida, 1 in Kentucky, 1 in Virginia, 1 in New York and 1 in Connecticut. Total of 11 states so far.

Which leads me to my book. Doubleday sent it back and asked if I could make it more general to cover the whole U.S. and then resubmit it.

This is a definite shortcoming of my manuscript but one that almost defies correction when dealing with these later bottles that we are digging and these are the bottles that this *new* hobby is concerned with. There aren't enough historicals, bitters and the real old bottles to go around but most everyone can dig up patent medicines, some bitters, old sodas, beers, whiskies, etc. How to revise my book when each area has their own group of bottles is a problem but possibly I can find a compromise, *if* I can find the time. At least I didn't get a flat reject and I appreciate Doubleday's consideration and offer to take a second look. With the way our hobby and our club is growing, now would be the time for a book such as mine.

Carol Farrell recommends "Lore of Our Land Pictured in Glass," Bessie M. Lindsey, Vol. I, Waggoner Printing Co., 1948. Describes and pictures 23 bottles and many other glass items.

Mr. Gardner told me in a recent letter that Van Rensselaer told him years ago that he (Van R) was going to make him (Mr. G.) the biggest bottle collector in the country. Van R. may not have had too much to do with it but at least Mr. G. did become the biggest collector.

Nice letter from the Kubick's. They found a Hostetter's Bitters with a paper label. "Web's Wild Cherry Wine and Iron Tonic." That was before the Federal Law Forbid days.

Good to hear from Mrs. Sheehan again. Has loaned her "Pontils" to friends in Red Bluff who have collected 500 bottles since being "infected" last fall. Lucky people, we haven't dug 50 bottles since I got the club by the tail (or vice versa) 2½ years ago. Not jealous – just envious.

Tom Neil received a letter from the Bergs giving their change from Florida to Virginia. She tells of all the bottles the hurricane brought in to shore and buried. She is interested mainly in bitters, inkwells and medicine bottles with "crazy" advertising. She is a trader. Watch these western "horse traders," Dorothee, but remember they do a lot of digging in hard adobe, not in real soft beach sand. Address: Comdr. R. A. Bergs, 1802 Adams Rd., Bayside, Virginia.

Letter from Mary Cowan, Bishop, wishing people there could start a club. I sure think you folks should – there are enough of you and you certainly have the bottles. You must have taken back a lot of applications from the show, Mary. Quoting from one of those applications: "I am just a beginner, but have already secured some real 'goodies'! – I have 'got it' bad (worse than love)." Ed. Note: Frank, how do you feel about the hobby?

George A. Austin, Scarsdale, N.Y., friend of Mr. G.'s, visited the Scroggins recently. He has a fabulous collection of flasks and they were very impressed with his knowledge of glass. We Westerners have a lot to learn. Sorry you couldn't have made one of our meetings, Mr. Austin; you could have told us a lot.

I note in "American Glass" that Lawrence Southwick, with two other men, established the third glass house in America. Mrs. T. is a descendant and we have the "Genealogy of Descendants of Lawrence and Cassandra Southwick." This book was published in 1881 in Salem. Quoting, "Lawrence Southwick...We do not find any mention of his name in the public records of Salem until 1639, when he and his family were admitted as members in the First Church of Salem, and two acres of land were given him by the town of Salem to carry on the business of manufacturing glass and earthenware. There is a tradition that he was one of the first to manufacture glass in America. This two acres was called glass-house field, as there were two others engaged in the same business and the land is so designated today on the records although the manufacture has long ceased."

463 pages and 8 generations later their book gets to Mrs. T.'s grandfather. I guess her love of glass has been handed down for 10 generations.

How would you like to be able to read in one place some *generalities* that would help you date bottles? Sure, from about 15 sources this can be done, but wouldn't this help?

    Free Blown w/Pontil Mark — from way back thar to 1860
    Free Blown w/smooth base — 1800 to 1860
    Blown in Mold, Applied Lip, w/Pontil Mark — 1815 to 1850
    Blown in Mold, Applied Lip, smooth base — 1850 to 1903
    Turn amethyst color in sun — 1880 to 1914
    Automatic Bottle Machine — 1903 on
    "Cures," "Specifics," etc. ceased about 1913
    Alcohol and opiates in P.M. contents ceased about 1913
    "Federal Law Prohibits...etc." — 1932 on

Well, at least I had the courage to put it down simply in one place *as a generality*. I am hoping for some constructive criticism. Also answers to where these items fit in.

    Graphite pontil — dates used, how and why?
    3 piece mold — when?
    "Crimp top" type lip, but on applied lip bottle — when?
    Inside screw top — when?
    Outside screw top — when?

Let's hear from you researchers.

Thanks, Lavine Layton, for your poem "Resolutions of a Bottle Bug" which I am including.     *J.C.T.*

### Resolutions of a Bottle Bug

My New Year's Resolutions
    for Nineteen Sixty Two
Find bigger, better bottles
    That's what I will do.
I'll sharpen up my digger
    I'll exercise, with care
I'll be in shape and all prepared
    To Hunt most anywhere.
When Bottle Huntin' Season
    Comes along with Spring
Joyfully I'll take the Trail
    To see what this year'll bring.

I think I've learned the lesson
    "Collecting To Restrain"
Still — might be wise to add it
    To this Resolution thing.
For way back there in Sixty

And even Sixty One
    When first the Bug had got me
And fever had begun,
    Then, every colored bottle
Found, looked good to me
    And every one I found, I carried
Home, so carefully.
    Now I'm a wee bit wiser
And know a little more
    About the places I should look
And what I'm looking for.

I also know this next one
    Is gonna bother me;
To sort and weed my bottles out
    But, it's just gotta be,
Because I've just no room left
    For new ones, and I know

I'll never stop collecting
So, some will have to go.
The poorest of the Colored,
Too many of one kind,
The common and the nameless
No matter how I mind
The parting with my First Founds
This thing, I have to do,
I must make room for my New Finds
Of Nineteen Sixty Two.

And now, I have another
In fact, a number more
But these aren't meant for me alone
I also make them for
All those who love, as I do,
To take the Bottle Trail.
I hope that they will all approve
And follow without fail,
No matter where the trail leads,
No matter where its end,
To act with care and courtesy
And leave behind, a Friend.

To close gates when requested
Be careful as to fire,
Cross not Forbidden Property
Nor crawl beneath the wire
Unless we've asked permission
If trespass signs are there,
And all too well, we know for sure
They're posted, everywhere.

Try not to be destructive
Nor leave a mess behind.
And if, along the Trail we tread
Deserted homes we find,
To never force a locked door
Nor one that's nailed up tight,
To "Let Our Conscience Be Our Guide"
No Matter what the sight.
We might see thro' a window
Some treasure from the past,
Perhaps an old and colored lamp.
Hold to that Conscience, Fast.

It just might be, the Owner
Plans to come again
To claim that which he's left behind.
So bear it with a grin
As we go on along our way
Our huntin' day most o'er,
With nothing done which might offend.
Of That, let's all be sure.

Friend Bugs — with what I've written
I hope you'll all agree
And join my Resolutions
With your good company.
If we'll all do our utmost
To see them carried thro'
We'll have Bigger, Better Bottling
In Nineteen Sixty Two.

*Lavine Layton*

## XXIV
## 185 Families in Club at this Point
## 55 Local
## 130 Out-of-Town

April, 1962

Joe Kelley reported on the Committee for the Redevelopment Area, saying that they were hoping to get permission to dig there, as a group, and assuring the Redevelopment Agency that we would not take advantage of their permission. Gene Stodgill volunteered to contact the Redevelopment.

Since John Tibbitts says the officers of the Bottle Club are responsible in the event of any lawsuits to the tune of $100,000 and liable for damages, we will have Liability Insurance and also, for the benefit of of digging on 2 Street, a "Hold Harmless agreement" for the Redevelopment Agency.

Wili Vidak claims our lending library is so good no one returns the books they borrow. (Good?) — Returned at end of meeting. L.S.

Our Guest Speaker for the evening was Mrs. DeWitt Nelson, who brought part of her collection of early American pressed glass. She demonstrated the use of glassware and fabrics as decorator pieces. *Everyone* enjoyed her talk which was cast with a good deal of humor and even the men were standing in the aisles for a better view of her artwork.

by Barbara Keskeys, Secretary

## THIS AND THAT — J.C.T.

Here it is, Easter Sunday morning — and a beautiful day. I was out in the back yard before breakfast and heard the unmistakable sound of geese overhead. Looking up, I found them; two groups, very high, honking their way north. These two big lopsided V's brought back to my mind the many mysteries and wonders of life, and made me think of some lines of Browning:

> The year's at the spring
> And day's at the morn;
> Morning's at seven; The hillside's dew-pearled;
> The lark's on the wing; The snail's on the thorn;
> God's in his heaven — All's right with the world.

A few replies received from my questions in last issue. Quoting Mr. Gardner, "I have a Whitney Glass Co. quart with inside threaded mouth and the cap is marked Pat Jan 1861." "I have a threaded mouth with cap on a Steigel type engraved tea caddy probably made in the 1700's"... most of the old rectangular brandy bottles bearing various enameled decorations carried pewter collars applied to fir screw caps so this places their use early in the 18th century."

From the 1670 Tavern — The Whittemores: "Glass turning amethyst. The most famous windows and panes-around-doors on venerable Beacon Hill in Boston, that have *really* amethyst coloring date back way beyond 1880... in fact to the 1700's we are told." "H.H. Hay and Son, Portland, Maine... and still going, though possibly under a different corporate name. They were very famous manufacturing pharmacists and druggists for years with many special products exclusive to them. It was founded in 1841." All good info — thanks to both of you.

Like to introduce you people to the "professional" who now types and prints the Pontil for us. She is Mrs. Cleona Howard and does a very nice job, especially so when you consider the scribbled, mixed-up notes I give her to work from. The first time I went to see her she drug out an amber Poland Water "Mosts" bottle. This just happened to be the issue I was quoting Mr. G. on that bottle. She has since shown me a few other bottles she had put away. Careful, Mrs. Howard, or the "boggle" bug may bite you if you don't watch out. Boy! was she apologetic about the bobble she made on "bottle" in the last issue.

Two more quotes from Mr. Gardner: "Does seem as if some of your members might make a trip east and get a chance to see my collection. After all there is a lot of pleasure in owning these treasures but it really is more fun to show them off to an understanding audience. Ken Wilson, Curator at Sturbridge, was down a couple of weeks back to take pictures of some of my glass. He is working on an article on Connecticut Glass for Sturbridge. They publish a Journal every little while covering the field of new discoveries in glass and while it costs $5 it is worthwhile and well worth it."

"Eventually we will get out to the coast and we will really have a wing-ding. I have so many correspondents out there that seem like old friends it will be a pleasure to meet them face to face."

The first year this club operated I received from 10 to 30 letters a week, asking about bottles and/or the club. I sure fell in love with those few who were considerate and enclosed a self-addressed stamped envelope for reply. It's a little thing — but important to a busy person. Remember this when you write to anyone with questions.

Understand about 25 members were at the first organized "dig" in the Redevelopment Area last Sunday. No great finds but a few nice bottles and a good time by all. Boynton, Fountain and Stagners came down from Quincy for this...dropped by here first, sure glad to see Alice recuperating so quickly from her surgery.

Bea recommends: "The Toadstool Millionaires" by James Young, $6.00. All about patent medicines. Also from Bea — a clipping from "100 Years Ago" column — "Florida Water, a rare perfume made from living flowers, is now available at S.C. Shaw's in our city. This wondrous liquid not only delights the nostrils but also removes headaches and faintness when applied to the temples, and eliminates rashes, tan and blotches when rubbed upon the skin."

Letter from Kubiks in Fresno stating they would like to start a Fresno branch of ABCA. Will send you our Constitution and By-Laws, Mrs. Kubik. Aside from what this will tell you, about all you would have to do would be to get an article with pictures in the Sunday Fresno Bee — then *get out of the way.*

A word of advice to all Associate Clubs. Keep it simple, keep it informal, don't read notes of previous meeting, and don't get all wrapped up in Robert's Rules. These clubs are "fun" clubs, not business clubs. If any members try to herd you down the Robert's Rules path, ignore them; the rest of the club will be behind you. The club meetings should be devoted almost entirely to displaying bottles, talking about bottles and glass, and meeting and talking with other bottle collectors. In the first two years of this parent club, when I was "president," I only called for three votes. On all other matters I acted as a benevolent dictator and kept the meetings for fun. Lee is doing a good job in this respect also.

Received the 3/15/62 meeting notes of the Shasta Antique Bottle Collectors. Noticed quite a few familiar names in the notes. Good to hear of you. They discussed our Constitution and By-Laws and objectives and decided to request permission to affiliate with us.

Alice Osborn, Secy., closed the notes with "There were 29 people attending and all were either talking bottles or trading bottles. It was a real good meeting."

Received the notes of the 5th (Feb.) and 6th (March) meeting of the Fallon Bottle Club. 22 present in February and 28 in March. They ask me about a brown bottle reading on the front, "Upper Bluelick 1770 Water" and on the back "Jas. W. Pierce, Proprietor, Maysville, Ky." I have seen one of these and heard something about it, but I can't remember a thing now. Help, please!

In their March meeting, Bob Ferraro presented a program showing Mr. G.'s slides and pictures. If many more of us borrow these pictures, they will become some of the best travelled pictures in the world.

Bought a new Almanac the other day that I haven't quoted from before. "Radway's R.R.R. Almanac and Guide to Health 1881." It advertises Radway's Ready Relief, Radway's Regulating Pills, and Radway's Sarsaparillian Resolvent. One testimonial naming all three products was dated 11/30/1868. The RRR was a Counter-Irritant, a Disinfectant, a Diffusive

Stimulant, an Antacid, a Diaphoretic, an Antispasmodic, a Rubefacient, an Anteseptic, a Sudorific, an Anodyne, a Nervine and Tonic. I haven't had need for some of those cures for a long time. Anyone that needed one of their other two products must have been a hypochondriac.

Also, just bought several Old Farmer's Almanacs, but didn't find too much to interest me, not being an old farmer. The poem for this month in 1896 — Longfellow:

*Enjoy the spring of Love and Youth,*
*To some good angel leave the rest:*
*For Time will teach thee soon the truth,*
*There are no birds in last year's nest!*

This must have been before anyone collected bottles 'cause it's pretty darn good in the summer and fall, too. The only bottled medicine advertised therein was Wistars Balsam of Wild Cherry which was good for Coughs, Influenza, Bronchitis, Whooping Cough, Croup, Consumption, and all Lung & Throat Troubles.

I think the cutest bottle we have in our collection is a little ¼ pint amber "pumpkinseed" flask we bought from Mr. G. On the front it has a circular wreath design and reads *Pap's Picnic's* (Plate #11). The bottom — S.C. CO. Anyone able to tell us something about it?

Another one that's got us curious, Mr. G. It's a GX-32 and McKearin only goes to GX-31. Amber pint flask, Eye in a Star and A.D. on one side, Rev.-Arm. and something in a Star and CRJA. SMBB??

Hope to give you all answers on above in next issue. Will also report on our experiments on melting glass in a "copper enameling" kiln. Have already produced some pretty exciting things and had lots of fun. As soon as we know what can be done we want to share this with you. Is real clean fun for we elder bottlers that can't dig as deep as we used to.

J.C.T.

## XXV
## Never Chew a Raw Oyster

June, 1962

In the last Pontil the Fallon Club had a question on a bottle "Upper Bluelick 1770 Water." The one I remembered belongs to Virginia Lewis. It reads on front "Bluelick Water" and shows a deer. On the back "Hamilton Gray & Co. Proprietors, Maysville, Ky." She wrote back there and found that this was a mineral water spa that was very popular at the turn of the century.

Mr. Gardner replied to my question on our GRJA (eye) flask: "You ask about the GRJA flask. It is pictured on plate 251 of Mac's book and has always been an unsolved puzzle, some think it is Masonic and others Odd Fellows or the United Workmen, but nothing definite has been discovered as to what it actually is. Among the flasks I purchased from the McKearin collection were a number, especially in the violin group that had unlisted numbers on them. Evidently as Geo. found unlisted specimens he gave them new numbers for use in a planned revision of the book. It is possible his daughter Mrs. Powers who is nearing completion of a new book may include his new numbers."

PLATE 13. Left to right. FREEBLOWN SPECIMENS.

- 10½" high, chestnut, dark amber, FBOP.
  Only 3½" thick at base and tapers in gradually to neck.
  7¼" wide at center of body.

- 11½" high, wine, olive green, FBOP.
  High tilted over kick-up with rough pontil scar about 2/3rds up.
  Pitkin type stretch marks on neck slightly swirled to left.

- 7¾" high, ovoid flask, pale green, FBOP.
  Body 2" thick with shoulder tapering in to neck.
  3¼" wide at center of body.

- 5¼" high, chestnut, light olive green, FBOP.
  Body 2½" thick near base and tapers in gradually to shoulder.
  3½" wide at widest part of body.

PLATE 14. Left to right, back. MISCELLANEOUS.

- 7½" high, round, green, BIMAL OR ABM?
  Seams go all the way to top but lip appears to have been broken off and rough ground.
  F — BABCOCK HAND GRENADE NON-FREEZING
     MANF'D BY FIRE EXTINGUISHER M'F'G. CO.
     325-331 S. DES PLAINES ST., CHICAGO

- 6¾" high, round, blue BIMAL OR ABM?
  Same as Babcock.
  On belt around middle — HARDENS HAND GRENADE FIRE EXTINGUISHER

- 9¾" high, 6 sided cathedral, cobalt blue, ABM.
  Around base — CARTER CARTER (2 letters in each panel).

  Front.

- 5¼" high, purse flask, cobalt blue, BIMAL.
  F — WHARTON'S WHISKEY 1850 CHESTNUT GROVE (in circular chain link)

- 5½" high, purse flask, amber, BIMAL.
  F — J.N. KLINE & CºS'  AROMATIC DIGESTIVE CORDIAL (in oval wreath of leaves)

PLATE 15. Left to right. CHARACTERS.

- 7" high, clear turning SCA, BIMAL.
"The Jester." Has butterfly on chest, small dog sitting up between legs in front, and appears to be stand-sitting on a log behind.
- 11" high, black (actually very deep amethyst), BIMAL.
"Russian Bear." Doesn't appear to have feet on front legs but the claws are there. Figure stippled to represent fur.
NO Embossed Writing. California collectors will recognize resemblance to "Smokey." Nearly identical bottles are found in clear glass with white overlay or with black overlay; also with Russian writing on them; also with "Federal Law Forbids etc."; also with label of Kummel.
- 8" high, light bright green, BIMAL.
"Sad Dog." Green cast is almost flourescent.
- 10¾" high, golden amber, BIMAL.
Flowing Beard "Moses" with staff and head turned slightly to right.
F — POLAND WATER (each word vertical just above toes on each foot).
B — POLAND MINERAL SPRING WATER (around monogram "P M S")
    H. RICKER & SON'S PROPRIETOR'S (Next to base)
- 7" high, turned SCA, BIMAL.
"The Hessian Soldier." (I call him 'Little Napoleon').
Piled up bunch of cannon balls between legs both front and back.
- 8¾" high, amber, BIMAL.
Waist up "Dutchman" holding pipe in hand. Some call him "Toby."
B — VAN DUNK'S / GENEVER  TRADE MARK  WARE & SCHMITZ

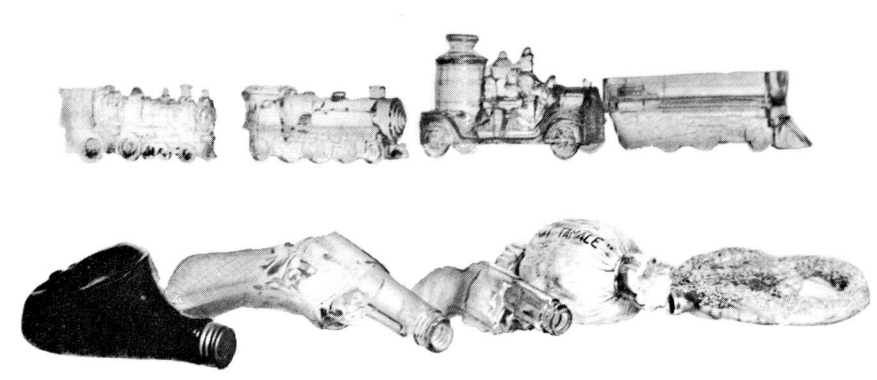

PLATE 16. Top left to right. CANDY CONTAINERS.

- Train Engine
- Train Engine
- Steam Fire Engine
- Open Top Train Engine

Bottom left to right. OBJECTS & CANDY CONTAINERS.

- Ham. Amber.
- Revolver.
- Revolver.
- "HOT TAMALE" (ceramic)
- Pretzel. (ceramic)

Here's another quote from Mr. G. and I guess we had better start calling our punkin seeds by their right name — Picnics. "Among dozens of old bill heads I have from various glass houses, mostly from the last quarter of the 19th Century (such as the photostat enclosed) are several listing the so-called Picnic bottles or "punkin seeds" as they are apparently called out there. One from Maring, Hart & Co., Bellaire, O. illustrates and identifies by the name Picnic these canteen shaped bottles, also another type which has flat side panels and a high rib on the edges called a Shoo Fly. The bill is dated Oct. 8th 1886. Agnew & Co. of Hulton, Pa. in 1894 was offering these Shoo Fly flasks as well as similar flasks with diamond designs on the sides and plain square pickle bottles. Others show the squat, cylindrical sodas with practically no necks which had wire stoppers in the neck dated 1900 and 1905."

The photostats he enclosed was of a letter dated 3/8/1878 and the letterhead reads "Office of Hero Glass Works, Hero, Gem, Hero Improved, and Crystal Porcelain Lined Fruit Jars. Factories at Philadelphia and Lockport, N.Y." It also shows four canning jars, "The Hero," "The Gem," "The Pearl" and "Porcelain Lines." The letter told about having contracted for 150 moulds @ $11.50 for quarts and $13 for half gallons.

Very interesting info — Thanks, Mr. G.

Nice note from Bea Boynton. She, Alice Fountain, the Barney Martins and the Stagners spent two days digging in Virginia City. Said the Martins and the Stagners did real well but that she and Alice just couldn't do that deep digging. She said, "Barney was at least 12 feet below the rim of the dump." That's too much for me, too, Bea. About two feet is my limit these days; beyond that it ceases to be fun.

Here's a bit of Owl Drug and Wakelee's history via Kate Georgi and written by Don and June Kreiss. They are quoting their uncle who is 87 and an old San Franciscan. "You wrote the names of the Owl Drug Co. also Wakelee's. As far as I know the Owl opened its first store in the Parlan Building on Market Street. It was given the name *Owl* because, in its early days, remained open all night. It was the first drug store, within my knowledge, that carried many lines of merchandise not in the drug line — such as you find drug stores of today. They advertised "Cut-Rates" and were the pioneers, on the Pacific Coast, of their kind of drug store. Later on they were bought out by a financial syndicate who then opened stores all over California. They are now a part of the national chain of stores that trade under the name of Rexall. Their main offices are here in Los Angeles in a huge and imposing building. I have been in it. I had occasion to go there when I was representing eastern factory lines. Wakelee's Drug Stores were an old institution in San Francisco. We used to get our supplies from their branch store. That was before the fire and earthquake, located at the northeast corner of Sutter and Polk Sts. That location is now occupied by Foster's Restaurant." Thanks, Don and June.

Did you know that from 1500 BC to about 100 BC glass bottles and jars were made by the sand core technique. The sand or clay was shaped on a metal rod and then dipped and redipped in molten glass. When completed, the sand core was scraped out. About 300 BC the blowpipe was discovered and this brought about a new era of glass making. This technique advanced so rapidly that the first four centuries AD are known as the First Golden Age of Glass. The next technique to be developed was the use of the mold along with the blowpipe and this early technique continued with only minor changes right up to 1903 AD. Let's summarize this:

    From 1500 BC to 300 BC — Sand Core
    From 300 BC on — Free Blown
        to 1903 AD — Mold Blown
    From 1903 AD on — Automatic Bottle Machine

I think many of us are of the opinion that most of the alcoholic "patent" medicine and bitters were sold mainly to the men. Tain't so — at least much of the old advertising indicates otherwise. Quoting from a beautiful old Burdock Blood Bitters trade card: "Invalid Ladies!! This is for You. There are thousands of females in America who suffer untold miseries from chronic diseases common to their sex. This is due largely to the peculiar habits of life and fashion and the improper training of girlhood. Then, too, the physical changes that mark the three eras of womanhood (the maiden, the wife and the mother), have much to do with their sufferings, most of which is endured in silence, unknown by even the family physician and most intimate friends. To all such whose hollow cheeks, pale faces, sunken eyes and feeble footsteps indicate nervous and general debility bordering on consumption, we would earnestly recommend that grand system-renovating tonic, Burdock Blood Bitters."

It is a shame you silent sufferers cannot obtain such a beneficial medicine these days.

Many of us who have dug in many of the old western dumps have pondered on the quantity of oyster shells. In the Comic Almanac For The Year 1886, I ran across this gem — "You should never chew a raw oyster. Just place him lengthwise across the edge of your tongue, elevate your chin a trifle, and after that you will have nothing to do but pay for him." Is this getting to be a lost art? Sample of the humor, "It isn't a great way to the end of a cat's nose, but it's fur to the end of its tail."

George Reiber just dropped by with the info Harriet got from Toot Garten on where we are going to camp in Virginia City on our June Field Trip. Here's Toot's directions: "It is only one mile from the Delta Saloon — go north — toward Reno, after leaving the north edge of Virginia City you go around curve on highway until you come to "End of 20 Mile Speed Limit" sign — 20 ft. beyond this turn right and go down dirt road. Follow this road around the hill for about a quarter mile and the mine dump or camp spot is on the immediate right."

Toot is going to put ABCA Signs up for us by 10 a.m. on June 23rd. The "camp out" is June 23 and 24. There are motels in Virginia City and Carson City for the less hardy (or less foolhardy). It's worth the discomfort of camping just to watch Toot cook his coffee from an old tin can. Toot warns of an open mine shaft at this camp site that only has a couple strands of cable fenced around it but as Toot so aptly puts it "which will bother no one if let along."

You know, fellow bottlers, I always thought Toot a real good friend, but I am going to quote his P.S. in his letter to the Reibers, then you be the judge. "P.S. On second thought, if that beer guzzling, off pitch crowd that kept the camp in an uproar most of the night at Summit City is going to have another 'sing along' we'd best set up a campsite about 3000 ft. in from the mouth of Sutro Tunnel."

As long as you didn't actually name the two culprits, Toot, I guess I can't stay mad. If we can just get a third one to join the two of us, with a guitar, we can keep on pitch this year and the tunnel will add the resonance we lacked out in the open. "Home, Home on the Range..." Mr. Gardner, do you play a guitar?

Warning to sleeping bag campers (that's what Mrs. T. and I are): June nights can be *awful* cold in that high country, so bring extra blankets, just in case. 'Tis far better to bring 'em and not need 'em than never to have loved at all...

We have recently added some nice eastern "sodas" (mineral water) to our collection. Among them are several from Saratoga, N.Y. This must have been quite a spa and we wonder about what dates these bottles cover. The ones we have are embossed (some splits, some pints, some quarts).

"Highrock Congress Springs — C & W — Saratoga, N.Y."
"*D. A. Knowlton — Saratoga, N.Y.*" — (Plate # 7 )
"Geyser Spring — Saratoga Springs — State of New York — The Saratoga Spouting Spring"
"*Hathorn Springs — Saratoga, N.Y.*" — (Plate # 7 )
"Saratoga Vichy Spouting Spring — V — Saratoga, N.Y."
"Congress & Empire Spring Co — C — Saratoga, N.Y. Congress Water"
"*Empire Spring Co. — E — Saratoga, N.Y. — Empire Water*" — (Plate # 7 )

Wonder how many more there were, or are? J.C.T.

## XXVI
## Now Have Members in
## 23 States
## 257 Families Altogether

THE PONTIL

ABCA                              September, 1962
Lee Scroggin, President           6737 - 51st St., Sacramento 24
Tom Brown, Vice President         1814 - 5th Ave., Sacramento 18
Tom Neil, Membership              3421 Palomar Way, West Sacramento
Elmer Lester, Program             4116 T St., Sacramento 19
John Tibbitts, Editor             3161 - 56th St., Sacramento 20

Here we go again after a two month "rest." Have shown the officers because there have been so many new members coming in this summer, both local and all over the U.S. Hello and welcome to all of you.

This summer has been the best ever for the local "bottlers." The field trip to Virginia City was enjoyed by many and produced a lot of fine old bottles -- some from the V.C. dumps and some from Gold Hill. Some of the folks camped out on the ground, some had trailers, some had tents and some used motels. It's hard to describe the fellowship and thrills and fun found on these trips. Try it some time — you don't have to dig to share the fun. Mrs. T. and I ran over for a day and a night and didn't dig or even scratch once, just visited and shared the fun. Didn't use Sutro's Tunnel — no guitar.

The Sacramento Redevelopment area in our old west end has really paid off, too. The excavations at the Macy site and the Wells Fargo site produced hundreds and hundreds of bottles as well as many new collectors. The bottle digging starts after the contractor stops excavating for the day or weekend. We were told it was not uncommon during the Macy excavation for 40 to 50 or more bottle collectors to be digging at once. We were too busy to look in at Macy's but did visit the Wells Fargo site one evening. There were about 30 people, each digging and scratching in his or her own little spot.

The finds at these two locations included open pontil, graphite pontil and smooth base. There were Bitters, Patent Medicines, Inks, Pottery, Cathedrals, Hot Sauce, Beers, Whiskeys, Perfumes, Sodas, etc., etc.

We spent a week "scrounging" around Nevada with Jackie and Lee Scroggins and Toot and Dorothy Garten. Not too many finds but lots of old sites and fun that goes with just thinking about the history involved. We tried Tonopah, Manhattan, Eureka and Austin.

Who left the two broken "schoolhouse" inks in the dump in the gully just west of Austin? Did you get any whole ones? They are sure beauties. A perfect one was dug in Sacramento this summer.

Dug up two beautifully etched and irridescent old amber bottles in Austin that are worth mentioning. One was a Hostetters and the other a beer. The Hostetters had a red and black label nearly rotted away and when I washed this off you can nearly read what it said in the etching on the bottle. The beer exhibits this same phenomenon also.

The first meeting after "vacation" held on 9/4, was very well attended. Many new members and guests were present. "Summer Finds" was the theme and many beautiful old bottles were on exhibit.

I showed the colored slides I took on our trip to Mexico. This included several in a glass "factory" in Tlaquepaque and several in the Avalos "factory" in Guadalajara. It's worth a trip down there just to see them produce the free-blown glass items using the methods and tools we used in our glass houses here over a hundred years ago. And — the girls are pretty down there, also! Viva la Mexico!

This club started in October, 1959, and since that time we have put out monthly notes. Good or bad, I have been responsible for most of the work involved in putting them out. There have been many requests for back numbers Mrs. T. and I have sent these out as long as we had some left. At the meeting on 9/4/62 I asked for, and received, permission to re-edit this material and publish it at my own expense. This will be a paperback booklet with black and white photograph plates. Think I will call it "CHIPS FROM THE PONTIL." Plan to include only the more meaty material.

May Jones, Bishop, has published a second book. This one is "The Bottle Trail Volume 2" — price $1.50. They may be ordered from the Chalfont Press, Bishop, Calif. and are probably available in many of the "bottle shops."

Bottle collecting as practiced here in the west has really come up out of the dumps. How many of you remember (only 3 years ago) when the only place you could find bottles to buy was on the back shelf or out of a box in the back of an antique shop or a junk store. Now every shop has a display of bottles for sale. Of course, the prices have gone up, too.

On the strength of this "upgrading" of our hobby, Mrs. T. and I rented a booth in the Annual Antique Show which ran for 10 days at the California State Fair. We moved our "Little Glass Shack" out there but wondered whether we really belonged in that class. We were very pleased with the response and interest shown in our exhibit. Even most of the general run public (no admission) were very interested. Other dealers in the show complimented us on the exhibit and were surprised at the interest in bottles in this area. We received a few snickers and several times heard: "I got a basement full of junk like that" — but on the whole, I repeat: "bottle digging has come up out of the dumps."

The Stodgill's loaned me an article on the evolution of the Coca-Cola Bottle. The first bottles used were the old 6 oz. Hutchinson stoppered bottles, with the wire hook that held the stopper in place protruding from the neck when the stopper was pulled up. The oldest one mentioned was dated 1900 and appears to read " — Electric Bottling — This Bottle Loaned Must Be Returned When Empty. Valdosta, Ga." The picture shows this Hutchinson to be the short neck heavy glass soda bottle that we dig so many of; not the prettier tapering neck soda. From this bottle they went to a crown cap within a few years but the familiar Samuelson design was not patented until 1915. They call the color of this bottle "Georgia Green" and reject bottles "Bums, Crocks, and Scuffies." Very interesting, Gene and Adele — thanks.

Lou Denchfield loaned me the July 1962 issue of Tideways — Port of Stockton. This tells of the new Owens-Illinois Glass Container Plant (*Great Scott!* a punkinseed flask sitting in a box right behind me just blew up! all by itself, and what a noise it made. Guess it just got tired but it sure made me jump.) four miles out of Tracy. Maybe the club can arrange a field trip there some Saturday? They make 120 tons of glass containers daily. In addition to the interesting article on how the Tracy plant works there is a short article on early glass making. Try writing to Olympics Organization, 807 N. San Joaquin St. Suite 215, Stockton, Calif. for a copy. Thanks, Lou.

The March 1962 issue of Mexico News has a two-page pictorial article on the Avalos glass house in Guadalajara. One picture of a beautiful bottle and a beautiful girl has a caption "The less you can expend There's always a nice lovely thing cheap as you can pay." No comment — except they still use English better than I do Spanish.

Pat and Cal Mendonca of Carson City loaned me an 1891 Guide for Humphrey's Veterinary Specifics. Don't know if these bottles are showing up but if so, AA cured fevers, BB for tendons, CC for glands, etc. through JJ for digestion. It also advertises Humphries Homeopathic Specific 28 for nervous debility and Humphries (Witch Hazel) Marvel of Healing. According to the 50 years advertised, the company must have started in 1841.

In one of the last issues I listed some of the beautiful Saratoga Springs bottles we have and questioned how many there might be. B. Barbin, Amsterdam, N.Y. lives just 30 miles from Saratoga and sent the following info. There were many springs in this area. Saratoga's glory was in the gay 90's — Spas, hotels, race track, betting, etc. Water is all naturally carbonated — "mostly tastes terrible altho I do like Hathorne." "Some people, especially those living in or near Saratoga, make Saratoga bottles only their collection hobby." Saratoga is the oldest continuous race track in the U.S. New York State is now financing Saratoga. Thank B., Elizabeth.

I picked up out of McKearins the fact that about 1865 the Congress and Empire Spring Co. acquired a glass works about 8 miles out of Saratoga and moved it to the Congressville section of Saratoga. No wonder those green bottles are so beautiful — they made their own.

Tom Brown did some research in old Sacramento City Directories and came up with: "Dr. Renz's Celebrated Herb Bitters. The Grand Specific of all diseases arising from an impure state of the blood or diseased Stomach. Try it! Try it! Try it! J. Renz, Prop., 222 J St. Sac." Ad appeared 1857 to 1874.

Ad in 1870: "Dr. Henley's Celebrated Wild Grape Root Bitters. IX L is the best tonic in the world. Is a sure cure for Dyspepsia. A safe remedy for indigestion. Sold Everywhere. L. Gross & Co. Sole Prop., 518 Front St., S.F."

He also found references to "Dr. Dake's Ague Bitters" (1860) and "Merrell's Wild Cherry Bitters" (1863-64). Anybody have either of these? Thanks very much, Tom. Anyone who has tried researching directories will appreciate the hassle you went through.

A few issues back I quoted an ad on Plantation Bitters found in an 1865 Harper's Weekly. Today I received a 4 log Plantation with both the front and back labels intact and part of a 2¢ revenue stamp. The front label reads "Drake's Plantation Bitters or Old Homestead Tonic. (picture of plantation) S-T-1860-X. Composed of pure St. Croix Rum, Calisaya Bark and other Roots and Herbs. — P.H. Drake & Co. New York." I'll repeat — the ST and the X in the glass and label must stand for St. Croix. From the back label "A waterglassful taken three times a day, will impart tone and cheerfulness to the whole system." Hic!

In July, Lee and I went to Columbia and gave a talk and displayed some bottles to the Tuolumne County Historical Society. We were very well received. This is the third historical group I've been invited to now and in February the Sacramento Arrangers Guild have requested my "services." Yes, sir, folks — our hobby is coming up Up UP. *J.C.T.*

## XXVII
## Purple Bottle Awards

October, 1962

THIS AND THAT — *J.C.T.*

This October meeting was one of our best. Snow-maker Denchfield showed some wonderful slides of bottle collecting trips to many Nevada ghost towns. Maybe you could sell the snow you seem to induce and just buy your bottles, Lou.

Elmer Lester presented the Purple Bottle Award to members who had received injuries in the line of duty (bottle digging). Marie Huson, Harriet Reiber, Betty Denchfield and Edith Tibbitts received these awards. In addition to receiving these awards (a purple bottle with purple ribbon necklace) our President was very gracious and awarded them the privilege of running the next meeting.

Everyone brought and displayed "stuff 'n junk" collected while bottle digging. The displays were unique and very interesting.

Rick Wallace displayed his fine collection of "pepper sauces."

Bea Boynton sent me a copy of an ad on Siegerts. Quoting — "Angostura Bitters (Dr. J.G.B. Seigert & Sons) Ltd. Famous Since 1824.

Factory at George Street, Port-of-Spain, where the World-famous Angostura Aromatic Bitters and Siegert's Rums are produced. One of Trinidad's oldest industries and one of the very first to export finished products to the outside world." Thanks, Bea.

Any of you have a Siegert's Rum? or an 1824 Bitters? How many of you have noticed the two main variants in the older Siegerts? The base of one reads "Dr. Siegert Cd. Bolivar"; the other "Dr. J.G.B. Siegert & Hijos." I think the Bolivar is older — anyone know for sure?

We might kick bottoms around a little more. We have two Warner Tippycanoes. The bottom on one reads: "Rochester N.Y./Pat Nov. 20.83"; the other only "Rochester N.Y." (no "e" nor patent date). Which is older?

We have had S.O. Richardson Bitters with open pontil, graphite pontil and with smooth base. In this case I believe the open pontil the oldest (by the type of glass and lip) and the smooth base the newest with the graphite in between. I have asked before and will again — who can tell us about these "graphited" pontils if that is what they are? When was the process used, etc?

We have an *Old Sachem Bitters* (Plate # 3 ) and a Binninger barrel *Old Kentucky 1849 Reserve Bourbon* (Plate # 11 ). Both of these have open pontils. We have previously had these same two bottles with smooth bases. Can any of you make something of this?

Well, that's enough on bottoms except to say that the moral of this story might be — Keep your eyes open, you can never tell when a better bottom might show up.

A couple of years ago I think I told you about the little character bottle we found in the east. He's about $7\frac{1}{2}$ inches tall and a full figure of a fat little soldier with a high hat. We call him "*Little Napoleon*" (Plate #15 ). We gambled and put him on the roof and he has turned a nice light amethyst already. The other day we received his partner "*The Jester*" (Plate # 15 ). He, too, was clear so we have him out in the elements to see if he will color also. We brought Napoleon in so Jess will have a chance to catch up.

The Pittsley's of Napa sent me an interesting article on the Napa Soda Springs. Amos Buckman filed the first claim on the property on August 19, 1855. Quoting from the article, "One Charles H. Allen was the first to prospect with the water to determine its commercial possibilities. He manufactured a small zinc gasometer, being a tinner by trade, and with this collected an amount of gas. He installed pipes and so arranged them that the force of the water would charge a cylinder with water and gas at the same time. He brought the cylinder to Napa and attached it to a bottling machine and thus the first bottled Napa soda was turned out."

Tom Brown gave me what's left of an old Lilly order book that advertises their many fine drug products. Only two of the pictured bottles are of interest to us. One is the familiar fish bottle pictured side view and bottom view, both with cork end up and true base of bottle down. The flat part on the underside of the fish has a label reading in part "Cod Liver Oil." The advertising tells us, "A pure Norwegian oil in the distinctive cod bottles — a novelty that attracts and repeats — " "Make the most of this opportunity to build up a demand on a unique and distinctive item that is sold only in drug stores. Supplied only in one pint cod bottles."

So, if you have one of those amber pint fish bottles that resembles a carp, you probably have a Lilly cod bottle.

The other one is a Poison bottle best described by the advertising: "To safeguard against errors these tablets are molded diamond shape, and are put up in diamond shaped bottles with corrugated corners. The word "POISON" is conspicuous on both bottle and label." Many of you will recognize this as the small amber bottle that we dig in the not-too-old stuff.

Tom also researched the following info on local sodas:

| | |
|---|---|
| Boley & Co. 1856-62 | (Hugh) Casey & Cronan 1876-86 |
| (Owen) Casey & Kelly 1860-66 | Hugh Casey 1886-1904 |
| Phil Caduc 1855-81 | T. Blauth 1880-1904 |
| E. L. Billinger 1868-84 | T. Blauth & Co. after 1904 |
| (Hugh) Casey & (Hugh) Kelly 1873-75 | Casey & Kavanaugh 1906-13 |
| Postel & Schnerr 1882-92 | (Successor to Hugh Casey) |
| M. Cronan 1901-11 | C. Schnerr 1893-1911 |

Thanks for sharing this hard-earned info, Tom.

The Fallon (Nevada) Bottle Club sent us the notes on their first fall meeting. The Nevada Historical Society sent them a letter thanking them for the bottles they had donated to the museum.

Ned Kendricks found the two broken Schoolhouse Inks I mentioned in the last Pontil. He did not get a whole one. Lear Lewis did find a whole one in Virginia City last spring.

The Fallon group wants to officially be affiliated with ABCA. Starting with the next Pontil we will list all clubs and their addresses that wish to be so affiliated. Let me hear from the rest of you if you wish to be so listed. (Thanks, Jacque — nice notes to work from.)

We bought a bottle from a Bay Area antique dealer that is worth describing. It is BIMAL, light honey amber, $10\frac{3}{4}"$ tall, $2\frac{1}{4}" \times 3\frac{1}{4}"$ base tapering to $2" \times 2\frac{1}{2}"$ at shoulder, old wavy glass, roped corners, front and back panels at top have fancy 3 window arch, side panels at top have fancy oval, front panel _Expectoral Wild Cherry Tonic_ (Plate # 4 ) left — Rohrer's, right — Lancaster, Pa. If it only said Bitters instead of Tonic, I could retire. Anyone have any history on this bottle or the product or the company?

Those of you with a _Yerba Buena Bitters_ (Plate # 3 ) may appreciate this little tidbit I found in a booklet on Indian Uses of Native Plants. It lists Yerba Buena (Micromeria chamissonis) under beverages and states, "Leaves dried for aromatic tea. This is the plant the original name of San Francisco came from."

While I'm in the book — The Blackfeet called Bitter-Root "Ax six sixie." The recipes for wild game included, "Pelican Eggs: First get the eggs. Boil till done." How's that for a practical recipe, Miss Crocker? Or, to use my corn —

> Scare-um Pelican, fly away
> Find-um egg, nest of hay,
> Boil-um done, recipe say,
> 3 Minute — or all day?

Which reminds me, Chief Screeching Train Whistle — did you know that old Sacramento had a Garten Gold Cure Institute Company. Cured addicts of dope, liquor and tobacco habits. Any relation?

SAFETY FIRST...Be ever aware and wary of "cave-ins" and/or bank "fall-offs." Just now had a phone call about a local 14-year-old boy who yesterday was seriously injured while bottle digging and is in the hospital. The four "purple bottle" awards mentioned above could have been serious and there have been other close calls.
1. Never dig alone;
2. Never tunnel back in;
3. Never scratch or dig under a cut bank over 3 feet high;
4. Warn fellow diggers about unsafe acts.

No bottle is worth a life, and the life you save MAY BE YOUR OWN.

*J. C. Tibbitts, Editor*

## XXVIII
## Ten Bottle Digging Commandments

November, 1962

Notes from acting secretary Rene Knapp 11/6/62:

Ladies Night. Lee thanked everyone for the White Elephant Sale. $112 worth of bottles sold and money given to Garden Center. Lucy Traub Show November 14, at 2 o'clock, Garden & Art Center. Display of bottles. Bill Sherwood, Comm. Chairman for Redevelopment Area. Mr. Stoghill asked for permission not too successfully. Mr. Tibbitts closed property at 24th C. Willi Vidak on new library books asked members to borrow Bottle Books. Lee appointed Committee Chairman. New officers: Tom Neil, President; George Reiber, Vice Pres.; Secy., Rene Knapp; Treas., Lou Denchfield. John Tibbitts suggested nominations closed on new officers for 1963. Dec. 4 meeting at Buckboard, 6135 Stockton Blvd., 7 p.m., $2.60 adults, $1.45 for children under 12. Reservations to Lee before Nov. 18. Edith Tibbitts suggested each member send one bottle to Neva Markham, Box 903, Anderson, Calif. Lost entire collection of bottles in fire. Mary Heiss speaking on buttons: Pudding, Goldstone, Art Glass, Black Glass, watch crystals, etc. Book in library, complete button book. Paperweight buttons look exactly like paperweights.

THIS AND THAT − *J.C.T.*

Received a letter yesterday from Golden Horseshoe Bill Maccoun. He must have been born with that shoe in his mouth. Quoting his letter: "With much good fortune I found myself in New London on business! Tonight, while you were having a club meeting, it was a real thrill to see Charlie Gardner's collection. It would appear that in many areas he has a head start on most of us! Nuff said −" How lucky can you be?

However, Bill, I bet you and Mr. G. would have enjoyed the meeting. The ladies put on the program and all 90 of the people present were "rolling in the aisle" before they were through. First they had Karen Jorgenson read their Ten Digging Commandments for Husbands:
1. Dig no holes deeper than 20 feet.
2. Dig no more than 12 hours without a break.
3. Deodorize before entering the house after digging in old deserted privies.
4. All wives must be allowed to bring home *anything* they find.
5. All full bottles taken along must be shared.

6. All digging shall cease at dawn.
7. Replace "No trespassing" signs when leaving premises.
8. Give nothing away until inspected by the wife.
9. Open no beer until after 12:00 noon.
10. If you dig beyond 6:00 p.m., you must take your wife to dinner.

Karen then introduced her mother, Lillian Jorgensen, as the commentator for the "Fashion Show" some of the girls were putting on. Lillian came on as flamboyant as Diamond Lil would have — 2 foot cigarette holder 'n all.

Now I must digress for those of you that don't have teenagers and haven't heard the "Stripper" record and don't "dig" the implication. Let's see — maybe we can just say this music suggests and is used in certain entertainment spots while the "actress" is doing what she does while she is doing what the name of the song suggests.

Now — these girls were all dressed in some kind of a bottle digging costume and you never saw such a conglomeration in your life! They came out one at a time and "paraded" around while Lil described their costumes over the mike. The costumes and the "parading" I can't describe but they had us all howling. They were presented as:

1 — the luscious Fifi Lewis
2 — the bouncy beauteous Bubbles Scroggin
3 — that sweet Candy Bar Kelly
4 — the sensational Sunny Gaylord
5 — that ever lovin' Toots Tibbitts
6 — the tempestuous Tempest Storm Huson
7 — the lovely angelic Lily St. Anthony
8 — the darling of them all, Gypsy Rose Kelly

This last character was a real buxom, black dressed, long blond tressed gal carrying a fancy bejewelled 2 ended digging tool. He turned out to be Joe Kelly.

I sure wish every one of you could have seen this!

Received a real nice letter from the Edgar's, associate members who live in Marathon Shores, Fla. They live on Grassy Key which is about halfway between Key West and Key Largo. They have been collecting in the Keys for about 1½ years (2200 bottles) and take many real rugged trips prowling the Mangrove swamps and beaches. How does that sound to you city-bound slickers? Quoting from their letter, "We had a good laugh about your hobby coming up out of the dumps. One of our best sources of old bottles is a former dump in a swamp in Key West. It was covered over with sand and some bright soul discovered that by digging down from three to five feet you find many old and lovely bottles. During the winter (?) season, Dec. thru April, it is common to see heads sticking out of holes in this area and tourists going by ask 'What are those crazy people doing?' At the present time I tell them we are digging fox holes for the defense of the beach as about 500 yds. away are the guns — rockets — radar, etc. that the Marines have installed on Smathers Beach which you may have seen in the news."

Thanks, Edgars. Would like to trade you a western ghost town trip for a Mangrove swamp trip. Bet we would both enjoy it. Maybe someday we will.

Quoting from a note from Adele Reed, "Enjoyed the Oct. Pontil so much. Re the Angostura, etc. I believe our Ramsey's Trinidad Bitters is of that family, but a much older appearing bottle than Siegerts & Hijos or Sons. A heavier bottle than the Siegert Bolivar Cd. and a deeper olive green.

The entire Sept. '62 issue of "Lubrication" is devoted to Blown Glass. Texaco, Inc. publishes this. This belongs in every bottle collector's library. By means of a copy of these notes I will find out if we can obtain these either on an individual basis or a group basis. Will let you know next month.

Bea Boynton, Quincy, sent us a snapshot she took of the side of the old Roos Bldg. in Virginia City. In it is a painted sign, "Veni, Vidi, Vici. The Old Mexican Mustang Liniment For Man or Beast. It has Stood the Test for over Half a Century. Penetrates to the Root of Disease and Excels all Others." My Latin is more than a little rusty, but I believe the first three words translate to — I came, I saw, I conquered.

Just received an *Atwoods Jaundice Bitters* (Plate # 2 ) that I haven't seen before. It is 2¼ x 6¼, aqua, 12 sided, Bimal and reads on 5 of the panels *Atwoods / Jaundice Bitters / M. Carter & Son / Georgetown / Mass*. Does anyone know how this variant related to the *Moses Atwood* and the *Formerly Made By Moses Atwood* variants?

A week ago we bought a collection of over 300 *old* Bar Bottles and Decanters. I found myself thinking over and over "whatever possessed anyone to make a collection like that." Then I rather had to admit it was sort of like the pot calling the kettle black. I'll bet the fellow who made the collection had 10 times as much pleasure out of the hunting for and finding these oldies than he ever did actually looking at them. When you come down to it — how many of us would be bottle collectors if it were not for the thrill of the chase.

Just received a couple of Palmer Green beauties that maybe some of you eastern people can identify for us. They are 8" tall, Bimal, slender, small at base, tapering larger to shoulder which is only ¾" x 2", six sided. Base appears to read GIG Co. Front and back panel fluted.

Inasmuch as so many of you seem to be on a bitters kick, I will describe a couple of new ones we just received. This one sure looks like a patent medicine. It is 1¾ x 2½ x 8, Rect., Bimal, aqua. Front — Dr. Hoofland's German Bitters.

                B — C.M. Jackson Philadelphia
                L — Liver Complaint
                R — Dyspepsia Etc.

There's no beauty in that one but it does say *bitters* and could break the monotony of too many amber bottles.

The other one is a little more choice. It is 2½ x 9¼ bbl. shaped, Bimal, amber. On the front — *Dr. C. W. Robacks / Stomach Bitters / Cincinnati, O.* (Plate # 3 ). The barrel has 6 rings all the way around at both the top and bottom with 4 more rings on front side only at both top and bottom. It is a narrower bbl. than the Greeleys or the Bourbon and is a much lighter amber.

Can anyone tell us what our blue bbl. is? It doesn't say anything but it sure is a beauty. It is tall, Bimal, wavy glass, bluer than Jack Benny's eyes, and has 10 rings each top and bottom. Would like to know what label it carried.

I know many of you who have been picking up an old bar bottle or decanter as you could find them, either as a collectable or a conversation piece useable. Let me tell you a few basic things I have noted after going through 300 of them several times. They all kind of look alike, but —

> There are several grades
> Light and heavy
> Blown in mold or cut and polished
> Snap case or polished pontil
> Ground stoppers or not (decanters)
> Crystal-like glass or not
> White overlay letters or paint
> Gold leaf filled or gold paint filled.

They are all nice but if you are going to buy, at least be aware of quality. *J. C. Tibbitts, Editor*

## XXIX
## How Not To Clean Bottles

December, 1962

### THIS AND THAT — *J.C.T.*

Brother! If I ever get a Pontil out this time it will be a wonder...It's not just that it's a busy time of year (12/19) but Mrs. T. made like Marilyn Housewife and "straightened up and put away" all the junk 'n papers 'n letters 'n books 'n pamphlets etc., etc. that I keep around to help me. She's out tonight and I can't find ANYTHING — Ah, sweet mystery of life —

Bea Barbin writes that she has 5 different Atwood Bitters: "1st — blown, pontiled Moses Atwood, etc. 2nd — not pontiled. 3rd — M. Carter & Sons (wavy and old) like the original but no rough pontil. 4 — Rather clear, not near such interesting glass — formerly Made by, etc. 5 — Like 4 only a threaded top (The last type). All follow the same general shape." On some of the Saratogas she wrote: "The Congress Empire Spring bottles also come in an attractive old amberish shade — as well as that green. The amber really look older (they're not tho) as the amber-yellow color shows up the bubbles clearer. The Stoddard N.H. High Rock ones are exactly the same shape and size, only the green and amberish color is slightly different in color tone, and Stoddards seem to me more bubblish." Thanks, B.B.

Bea Boynton drove down from Quincy in the rain to spend a night with us, do some Christmas shopping, bring us a "I cut it down myself" tree (12 feet tall) (and she did) and to check into the bottle digging here. The present local bonanza is a complete square block in the old west end that is being excavated for the basement of a new building. It has produced some real good finds for about 10 days but they were about down to water level in a pretty sticky sort of gumbo. Well, the rains we just had, plus the one that persisted while Bea was here, didn't help — but we took her down Sunday morning. Nobody but a d--- fool would have walked down into that *mess* — so we did and ran into 2 more in there, digging. Yep, there was Joe Kelly and son Mike. They hadn't found anything yet but I am going to recommend that they be awarded an E Bottle — "E" for Effort. About every fifth step our feet would come up but our shoes wouldn't.

Bea brought us the Fall 1962 issue of The Feather River Territorial (American West Publishing Co., Oroville, Cal.) which has an article, "The Battle of The Bottle" by Bob Bennett. Quoting one paragraph, "And one of the richest sources of 'bottled gold' was a distinctly Butte county product known as Abietine — or Abietene — depending on whether it was from the vials of R.M. Green, an Oroville druggist, or from a botling plant of his arch rival and alleged imitator, D.F. Fryer, another local apothecary." Real good article with old advertising if you have either bottle or enjoy Patent Medicines.

If you enjoy this sort of reading, Bea recommends:

        In Camp and Cabin — Rev. John Steele
        Echos of the Past — Gen. John Bidwell
        A Diary in America — Frederick Marryat
        The Shirley Letters — L. Clapps & D. Shirley
        Emigrant Guide for Calif. — Jos. Ware
        Land of Gold — Hinton Helper
        Argonauts of Forty Nine — O. T. Howe
        A Short History of Calif. — Hunt Neville
        Diary of a Forty-Niner — A. J. Jackson
        3 Years in California — J. D. Barthwide
        El Dorado — Bayard Taylor
        Mining Camp — Chas. H. Shinn
        The Forty-Niners — Ewells & Peterson
        Miners & Molehills — F. Marryat
        Gold Rush — Sam Ware
        Ghosts of the Glory Trail — Nell Murbarger

I sure want to thank you two Bea B's for sending along this info. These gals may sound like they are shot, but they aren't — not even half.

Associate member Wm. G. Schoenberg is evidently quite a world traveler. He wanted a Lafayette bottle he found (France?) but had to buy 12 to get 1 and would like to help other members get a nice figure bottle and also get some of his money back. Cost, plus crating, plus shipping, plus customs adds to $12.00 per each.

Quoting a bit from his letter: "Dear John & Edith Tibbitts: Just returned home from another trip to sea. (Made Hawaii, Japan, Korea, Okinawa, Hong Kong and return). Received the Sept. Oct. issues of the Pontil, plus your mail order list. Enjoyed all very much. Keep up the good work, and keep 'em coming. They're great. Looking forward to making a trip up to your organization's meeting at least one time when I have to get off of this ship. Sounds very interesting, and I haven't been able to find very many bottle collectors, so would really enjoy meeting a few for a change. I should be home for my vacation around May or June." Thanks, Bill.

Mr. Gardner wrote and told us something of great import to all "soda" collectors, especially Saratogas. The April 1957 issue of New York History has a real fine article on "New York Antiques: The Springs, Glass Houses, and Bottles of Saratoga Springs, N.Y." by Fenton Keyes. We sent off $1.60 and got a copy but no reply to our inquiry about availability of more copies. So, try your luck.

General George Washington visited these springs in August of 1783 but was not successful in his attempt to purchase. At the end of this well written article is a "Collector's Check List of Saratoga Bottles." This describes 43 different Saratogas. Write to the New York State Historical Assn., Cooperstown, N.Y.

The following is quoted from a letter received from Mrs. Eunice Linderoth, Associate member: "Many rockhounds use acid in cleaning specimens and many do this cleaning in or around laundry tubs where bleach is used. The following Illinois Bell Telephone Co. safety bulletin is of vital interest: Witches Brew. Household Bleach, sold under various trade names is a solution of sodium Hypochorite. If *any acid* substance is added, it will release poisonous chlorine gas. Use of toilet bowl cleaner with bleach is very deadly and has been known to cause the death of one woman and serious illness of another person. (Vinegar and other acids will also liberate chlorine gas from bleach.)

"Never let children play with such compounds, they might accidentally combine the two and add them up to tragedy. The original item is from May 26 issue of Earth Science News. I think that while most of us are aware of the danger of combining bleach with an acid, we unconsciously forget when we are trying to remove a stubborn stain from a bottle." Thanks, Mrs. Lindroth. *Remember,* don't use bleach and anything acid.

Just bought an old (no cover) 1905 Recipe Book that is full of advertising. Only a little of it is of interest and I will quote some of those:

"Duffy's 1842 Cider Cup. A splendid substitute for Champagne Cup and especially suitable for those social evenings at home. To two quarts of Duffy's 1842 Cider, add one quart best claret wine, two sliced oranges, two sliced bananas, some stick cinnamon, sweeten to suit taste. Place a large piece of ice in a punch bowl and pour the mixture over it, serve in Champagne glasses with Maraschino Cherries." Sounds good. Wonder if related to Malt Whiskey?

"Ruby Mocha and Java Coffee." I just like the name — sounds real good.

"Coca Cola Pepsin Gum" And Coca Cola is written in the same familiar way it is on bottles?

"DON'T GROW OLD and dried up before your time. Water forms the basis of all the natural fluids of the body. The constant and plentiful use of SARATOGA VICHY will tend to keep you young, the joints supple, the skin unwrinkled. A sure cure for rheumatic gout."

"1852 — Hurlburt's Family Remedies — 1906."

"Hurlburt's Tracheal Drops."

"Dr. McMUNN'S Elixir of Opium. The pure and essential extract from the native drug. Possessing all the sedative, anodyne and antispasmodic powers of opium. Doctors prescribe it to produce sleep and composure, To relieve pain and irritation, nervous excitement and morbid irritability of body and mind. To allay convulsive and spasmodic actions, etc. Price 50 Cents."

"Mrs. Winslow's Soothing Syrup — 1840-1905 Sixty-Five Year's Record." No wonder we are digging them up with open pontils...

The best of everything to all of you in 1963.

*J. C. Tibbitts, Editor*